La Vern J. Rippley

Rainer H. Schmeissner

GERMAN PLACE NAMES IN MINNESOTA

Deutsche Ortsnamen in Minnesota

Cover Photo:

Sign at the entrance to the city of New Ulm in Brown County.

Foto auf der Umschlagseite:

Ortseingangsschild von New Ulm in Brown County.

ISBN 0-9622931-0-5

CONTENTS
Inhalt

Photographs:
La Vern J. Rippley: Nos. 1 - 43, 46 - 49, 51 - 55, 57 - 66.
Rainer H. Schmeissner: Cover photo, page 5, Nos. 44 - 45, 50, 56.

FIGURES

ÜBERSICHTSKARTEN

ILLUSTRATIONS

Drawings on pages 6, 9 and 49 by Francis Lee Jaques, adapted from
"Snowshoe Country", 1944, by Florence Page Jaques by friendly per-
mission of University of Minnesota Press.

Dedicated to all those
Who have left their old homeland,
And have found a new one
In the ”New World”.

Allen jenen gewidmet,
die ihre alte Heimat verließen
und in der „Neuen Welt"
eine neue Heimat fanden.

A "Minnesota Cross" in the "Old World"

In the 19th century, many Germans emigrated to the promised land - to America. In addition to the political reasons for leaving, there were those that involved primarily social unrest in the homeland. Peasant farmsteads could hardly support a family decently, thus the sons and daughters of farmers were compelled to seek their futures elsewhere.

The homesickness that resulted must have been intense. The soil of the homeland where they had spent their childhood could never be forgotten. A great many who found a new home in America sent money back home with the request that a cross be erected in their memory, one that would remind people for all time about the emigrants to America.

The inscription on the pedestal of one of these crosses that now stands in Eastern Bavaria has a direct reference to Minnesota. In 1874 there were three brothers by the name of Peter, Joseph and Michael Wagner who emigrated to America. On the journey there, one of the brothers died. The two others settled in Mankato and achieved financial success and respect there. To this day descendants of the Wagner brothers continue to live in Blue Earth County, Minnesota.

Ein „Minnesota-Kreuz" in der „Alten Welt"

Im 19. Jahrhundert wanderten viele Deutsche ins „gelobte Land" - nach Amerika - aus. Neben politischen Gründen waren es vor allem soziale Mißstände in der alten Heimat. Die Bauernhöfe konnten kaum eine Familie recht und schlecht ernähren, Bauernsöhne und -töchter waren also gezwungen, in die Ferne zu gehen.

Das Heimweh wird in den meisten Fällen groß gewesen sein. Die Heimaterde, dort, wo man die Kindheit verbrachte, blieb unvergessen. Nicht wenige, die in Amerika eine neue Heimat fanden, schickten daher Geld nach Hause mit der Bitte, zu ihrem Andenken ein Wegkreuz zu errichten, das für alle Zeiten an die Amerika-Auswanderer erinnern sollte.

Die Inschrift auf dem Sockel eines solchen Kreuzes, das in Ostbayern steht, hat einen direkten Bezug zu Minnesota. 1874 wanderten die Brüder Peter, Josef und Michel Wagner nach Amerika aus. Auf der Überfahrt starb einer der Brüder. Die beiden anderen siedelten sich in Mankato an und kamen dort zu Reichtum und Ehren. Noch heute leben Nachkommen der Wagner-Brüder im Blue Earth County von Minnesota.

Zum Andenken an
Peter Josef Michl
Wagner
die im Jahre 1874
nach Amerika
ausgewandert sind

Minnesota - Land of 10.000 Lakes

Minnesota - Land der 10 000 Seen

FOREWORD
Vorwort

In an upper Midwest state of the United States of America, with a name that goes back to the Indians (Minnesota = land of the sky blue waters) and in which many names still sound like their Indian origins, you might not expect on first consideration to be looking for German tracks and certainly not for names of places and towns of German origin.

But such a search is more worthwhile here than in scarcely any other state in North America. The North Star State (L'étoile du Nord), as Minnesota also likes to be known, was in fact settled rather densely by Germans. They streamed into this beautiful country that was established as a territory in 1849, at a time when the neighboring state to the East (Wisconsin) had already been elevated to the rank of a federal state of the Union. The "Frontier" as this border was called, functioned like a magnet for many immigrants from the Old World. Thus it is no wonder that as early as the second half of the 19th century, thousands of Germans who were leaving their homeland for various reasons, settled in this territory and brought to it their language and culture.

Over a hundred years later, and after two world wars which brought also on a prohibition of the German language and culture, German manifestations naturally have been reduced to the bare minimum. The third and fourth generations of immigrants have by now been assimilated by the dominant population while German customs and traditions have been almost entirely Americanized. To be sure many Minnesotans have German sounding family names, but very few still remember anything about their German origins. Hardly anyone still speaks fluently the language of their forefathers.

What has survived the ravages of time (for example two world wars), however, are the linguistic monuments in the form of place names. With few exceptions, the names have remained unaltered to this day. Approximately 200 German names having reference to cities, settlements, townships, and bodies of water have been pinpointed in Minnesota, which is a considerable number for any local region of North America. Only Pennsylvania is able to top Minnesota in this regard.

This modest text about the German place names in Minnesota would not have been possible if it were not for the standard work by Warren Upham, "Minnesota Geographic Names", which re-appeared in 1969 as a reprint of the 1920 edition by the Minnesota Historical Society in St. Paul. Warren Upham was a geologist, archeologist, and librarian, a man who had the tenacity to produce a volume that many decades after its publication in 1920 must still be considered as a timeless classic. His major contribution is that he created for Minnesota what one would love to find for every state in the Union. Admittedly, McArthur's "Oregon Geographic Names" (1944) and Gudde's "California Place Names" (1960) do approach Upham's accomplishment.

Upham's pioneer work is therefore the foundation for this volume. In his introduction Upham noted that "these German, Bohemian and Scandinavian names had great significance for the immigrants from those countries, who found their new homes here." Surely we can say today that such is no longer the case. Any association with the old homeland today is marginal, more often it is totally lost. To-day, many an inhabitant in a "German" town in Minnesota is not at all clear about his origins. Be that as it may, these German place names remain as linguistic monuments to the past. The task set for this study is to point out these place names and to explain them briefly. Where possible it will be shown what connection they have to places in Germany or in neighboring German-speaking lands (e. g. Switzerland and Austria). In this respect, "Müllers großes deutsches Ortsbuch" (1988) proved very helpful. On the basis of this reference work, it was possible to determine which German place names in Minnesota appeared likewise in the Old Homeland and how frequently they also appear either in the Federal Republic of West Germany or in the German Democratic Republic.

In einem Staat des hohen Mittleren Westens der USA, dessen Name indianischen Ursprungs ist (Minne'sota = Land des himmelfarbenen Wassers) und in dem viele Orte indianisch klingen, mag es auf den ersten Blick vermessen sein, nach deut-schen Spuren oder gar nach deutschen Orts- oder Platznamen zu suchen.

Doch die Suche lohnt sich wie in kaum einem anderen nordamerikanischen Staat. Der „Nordsternstaat" (L'étoile du Nord), wie Minnesota auch gerne bezeich-net wird, wurde nachgewiesenermaßen in großem Umfang auch von deutschen Sied-lern frequentiert, die massenweise in dieses herbschöne Land strömten, das 1849 erst zum Territorium erklärt wurde, zu einem Zeitpunkt, als der Nachbarstaat Wisconsin bereits den Rang eines Bundesstaates inne hatte. Die 'Frontier', wie man die Grenze nannte, die sich im 19. Jahrhundert immer mehr nach Westen und Norden schob, war für viele Einwanderer aus der Alten Welt wie ein Magnet. So ist es kein Wunder, daß bereits in der zweiten Hälfte des 19. Jahrhunderts Tausen-de von Deutschen, die ihre Heimat aus vielerlei Gründen verlassen hatten, sich in diesem Land niederließen, ihre Kultur und Sprache mitbrachten.

Über hundert Jahre später, nach zwei Weltkriegen, die zeitweise auch das Ver-bot der Ausübung deutscher Sprache und Kultur mit sich brachte, ist das Deutsch-tum auf ganz natürliche Art und Weise auf ein Minimum zurückgedrängt worden. Die dritte und vierte Generation der Einwanderer ist von dem großen Amerika as-similiert worden, Sitten und Bräuche wurden amerikanisiert. Zwar haben viele Be-wohner Minnesotas deutschklingende Familiennamen, doch nur wenige erinnern sich ihrer deutschen Herkunft. Kaum jemand spricht noch fließend die Sprache seiner Vorväter.

Geblieben und alle Unbilden der Zeit (z. B. Weltkriege) überdauert haben jedoch die sprachlichen Denkmäler in Form von Ortsnamen, die, bis auf wenige Ausnah-men, unverändert bis heute übernommen worden sind. Rund 200 deutsche Ortsna-men, bezogen auf Städte, Siedlungen, Townships und Gewässer, konnten lokalisiert werden, immerhin für Nordamerika eine immense Zahl. Einzig und allein Pennsyl-vanien weist mehr deutsche Ortsnamen auf.

Diese kleine Schrift über deutsche Ortsnamen in Minnesota wäre nicht möglich gewesen, gäbe es nicht das Standardwerk "Minnesota Geographic Names" von War-ren Upham, als Reprint erschienen bei der 'Minnesota Historical Society' in St. Paul. Warren Upham, Geologe, Archäologe und Bibliothekar, war der Mann, der mit Akribie und Ausdauer ein Werk erstellte, das auch viele Jahrzehnte nach sei-nem Erscheinen (1920) als zeitlos gültig angesehen werden muß. Sein großes Ver-dienst ist es, für Minnesota etwas geschaffen zu haben, was man seinesgleichen in den USA sucht. Allenfalls kommen seinem Werk McArthur's "Oregon Geograhic Names" (1944) und Gudde's "California Place Names" (1960) nahe.

Uphams Pionierarbeit ist auch die Grundlage für diese Schrift. Upham bemerkt in seinem Vorwort, daß „...diese deutschen, böhmischen und skandinavischen Namen für die Einwanderer jener Länder, die hier eine neue Heimat fanden, eine große

Bedeutung hatten..." Mit Sicherheit darf man heute sagen, daß dies jetzt nicht mehr der Fall ist. Die Verbindung zur alten Heimat besteht allenfalls nur noch in Bruchstücken oder ging gänzlich verloren, und mancher Einwohner in einem „deutschen" Ort in Minnesota ist sich dessen Ursprungs nicht sicher. Wie dem auch sei, die deutschen Ortsnamen blieben als sprachliche Denkmäler erhalten. Aufgabe dieser Schrift ist es, diese deutschen Ortsnamen aufzuzeigen und kurz zu skizzieren. Sie werden dort - wo es möglich war - in Beziehung gesetzt zu gleichlautenden Ortsnamen in Deutschland und den deutschsprachigen Nachbarländern (z. B. Schweiz und Österreich). Hierzu war 'Müllers großes deutsches Ortsbuch' (1988) eine wesentliche Hilfe. Aufgrund dieses Nachschlagewerkes konnte ermittelt werden, welche deutschen Ortsnamen Minnesotas auch in der „alten Heimat" auftreten und wie oft sie, sowohl in der Bundesrepublik Deutschland wie auch in der Deutschen Demokratischen Republik, vorkommen.

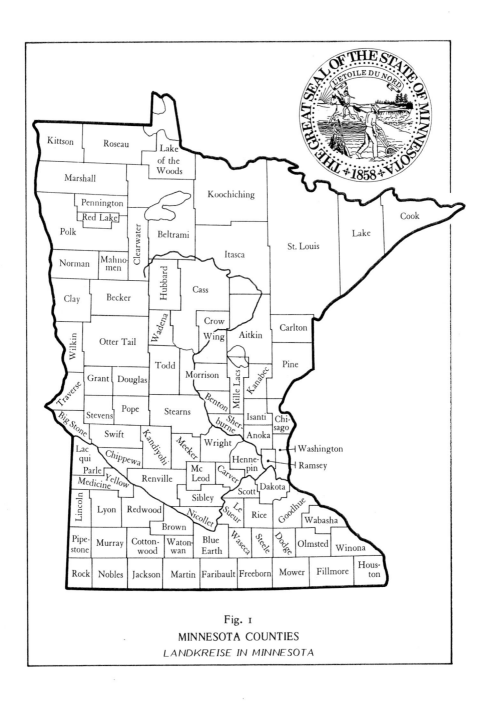

Fig. 1

MINNESOTA COUNTIES

LANDKREISE IN MINNESOTA

GERMAN PLACE NAMES IN MINNESOTA
Deutsche Ortsnamen in Minnesota

More than 700 geographic place names that appear on the map of North America can be shown to have a direct reference to the German origins of their founders. Among all of them, the name of the former capital city of Berlin is the most frequent, but numerous other German cities also have been memorialized on American place name signs, even though the contemporary inhabitants generally can no longer utter a single comment about their German city counterpart.

There are, however, American states in the Union in which German place designations are in evidence far in excess of the average. Among them are Pennsylvania, Illinois, Texas, Ohio, and Missouri - in particular Minnesota. This sounds paradoxical, for Minnesota especially, because it lies the farthest from the Atlantic coastline.

Surely it would be worth investigating what motives prompted German immigrants to prefer settling in this region between the Mississippi, Lake Superior and the Red River of the North. Some clues are rather obvious. Surely the benefit of a healthy continental climate (warm summers, cold and often snow-covered winters), had quite a bit to do with it. But this was certainly not the only, perhaps not even the primary reason. Good, stable economic conditions, a landscape that reminded the settlers of Europe, high quality educational possibilities, and outstanding farm land may have been other reasons which became known to prospective immigrants early on, that would allow Minnesota later to play first fiddle in the symphony of American states.

Since 1850 Germans leaving primarily from Southwest and Northern Germany, were immigrating into this region which at the time was quite forested. They claimed their land, founded settlements, built roads and in the process discovered a new home in the land of 10,000 lakes. Second to the Germans were the Scandinavians who settled here, and in far fewer numbers. Both peoples left their marks on Minnesota in a major way, which today is evident in the festivals, customs, traditions, and not least, in the geographic names.

It was perfectly natural that those people who had survived the long trip across the ocean were mindful of their old homeland when it came time to pick names. They selected well-known old German geographic place names (Munich, Berlin, Hamburg, Hanover etc.) or they supplied other designations such as the first or last names of the first settlers (Manfred, Hermann, Essig, Hoffmann, Schroeder, Stark, etc.).

Even though it may sound paradoxical, in Minnesota - as also in other American states in the Union with a lot of German names - the nomenclature of geography seems unreal. A breath of nostalgia wafts across the traveler's face in realizing that he can drive without having to cross any "Iron Curtain" whatsoever, from Berlin to Potsdam, from Munich (New Munich) to Weimar (Weimer), or from Hannover (Hanover) to Gotha. This geographic reality in the last quarter of the twentieth century, to be sure, exists only in Minnesota, not on the European continent.

Unfortunately the varying history of early settlement has not always been fully recorded on paper. Many of the places with glamorous-sounding names, on closer examination reveal little more than tiny specks in the middle of endless prairie land. Flensburg for example has scarcely more than 250 people (and they are almost all of Polish-speaking origins in German Silesia). Cologne (Köln) has only 500, while the city of Hamburg that lies in Minnesota comes in with a population of less than 400. On the other hand, New Ulm with its 13,000 inhabitants gives the impression of a good sized city. This town is also the only one that can still be characterized as "typically German", a feature that one looks for in vain in the other towns with German names. In New Ulm's architecture (e. g. the former post office, now the museum) as well as in its cultural remnants (The Herman Monument or for that matter, Martin Luther College) German features are in evidence to this day.

If we disregard the origins - or more accurately the remains - of this German aspect of Minnesota, there are however faint traces left which on closer examination can still be perceived. For example Flensburg, Minnesota is in essence a Polish settlement, more accurately a settlement of Americans of predominately Polish origins, whose inhabitants can in no way identify themselves with the German city of Flensburg in Schleswig-Holstein and as a matter of fact do not even know of the German city's existence. What can be said for Flensburg, perhaps can be said for a great many places in the "land of the sky blue waters" - these are historical town settlement place namens, nearly all of them from the 19th century. The founders and namers long since have been resting in their pioneer cemeteries. A walk through these is at the same time a passage through the past. It would be hard to get a better feel for the past of these communities than by a walk through these cemeteries. They illustrate and document the authentic pioneer spirit in a region that was strange to the newcomers. Whether they had arrived from Germany, Scandinavia, or Poland, they instinctively reached back to their native homelands to find place names, which they have preserved for all time on the maps and plats of the new nation.

Seen from this perspective, the German place names in Minnesota are nothing more than a breath of nostalgia from the past. Yet, they are inseparably tied to the settlement history of this state. The same holds true of course for the Scandinavian, Dutch, Polish and South European place names on the map of Minnesota.

Weit mehr als 700 geographische Ortsnamen finden wir auf der nordamerikanischen Landkarte, die eindeutig auf die Herkunft ihrer deutschen Gründer schließen lassen. Dabei ist der Name der ehemaligen Reichshauptstadt Berlin am häufigsten vertreten, aber auch zahlreiche andere deutsche Städte sind auf amerikanischen Ortsschildern verewigt, wenngleich ihre Bewohner oft gar keine Aussagen mehr über ihre deutsche „Schwesterstadt" machen können.

Nun gibt es amerikanische Bundesstaaten, in denen deutsche Ortsbezeichnungen überdurchschnittlich massiert auftreten. Zu ihnen gehören Pennsylvanien, Illinois, Texas, Ohio und Missouri - und vor allem auch Minnesota. Gerade im Falle Minnesota klingt dies paradox, liegt doch dieser Staat von all den eben genannten am weitesten von der Atlantikküste entfernt.

Es wäre sicherlich eine eigene Untersuchung wert, herauszufinden, aus welchen Motiven deutsche Einwanderer gerade dieses Gebiet zwischen Mississippi, Oberer See und Red River of the North bevorzugt besiedelten. Sicherlich war es die Gunst des gesunden Kontinentalklimas (warme Sommer, kalte, oft schneereiche Winter), die den Ausschlag dazu gaben. Dies war aber sicherlich nicht der einzige Grund. Stabile wirtschaftliche Verhältnisse, eine ans alte Europa erinnernde Szenerie, gute Bildungsmöglichkeiten und hervorragendes Farmland mögen weitere Kriterien gewesen sein, die sehr frühzeitig erkennen ließen, daß Minnesota später einmal im

Konzert der amerikanischen Bundesstaaten eine „erste Geige" spielen würde.

Seit 1850 wanderten Deutsche, vor allem aus Südwest- und Norddeutschland, in die riesige, damals noch fast völlig bewaldete Region ein, rodeten, bestellten ihre Felder, gründeten Siedlungen, bauten Straßen und fanden schließlich eine neue Heimat im Land der „10 000 Seen". Neben den Deutschen waren es in zweiter Linie Skandinavier, die sich hier niederließen. Beide Volksgruppen prägten das äußere Erscheinungsbild Minnesotas in entscheidendem Maße, was in den Festen, Bräuchen und letztenendes auch in den geographischen Namen deutlich wird.

Es war ganz natürlich, daß diejenigen, die den langen Weg über den großen Ozean glücklich überstanden hatten, insofern ihrer alten Heimat gedachten, indem sie altbekannte deutsche geographische Ortsnamen (München, Berlin, Hamburg, Hannover usw.) oder andere Bezeichnungen wie Vor- oder Nachnamen, z. B. die der ersten Siedler (Manfred, Hermann, Essig, Hoffmann, Schröder, Stark, usw.) auf die neue Heimat übertrugen.

So paradox es klingen mag, aber in Minnesota - wie in anderen amerikanischen Bundesstaaten mit häufig vorkommenden deutschen Ortsnamen - scheint die Geographie einfach Kopf zu stehen. Ein Hauch von Nostalgie überfällt den Reisenden, der, ohne den 'Eisernen Vorhang' überqueren zu müssen, problemlos von Berlin nach Potsdam, von München (New Munich) nach Weimar (Weimer) oder von Hannover (Hanover) nach Gotha fahren kann. Geographische Realität im letzten Viertel des 20. Jahrhunderts, allerdings nur in Minnesota, USA.

Leider ist nicht überall die wechselvolle Geschichte der ersten Besiedlung auf Papier festgehalten worden. Viele der Orte mit anspruchsvollen deutschen Städtenamen entpuppen sich bei näherem Hinsehen als oft nichts anderes als kleine Flekken inmitten einer schier endlosen Prärie. Flensburg zählt z. B. kaum mehr als 250, Cologne (Köln) nur 500 Bewohner, und Hamburg in Minnesota wird von nicht einmal ganz 400 Menschen bevölkert. Dagegen wirkt New Ulm mit seinen 13 000 Einwohnern schon wie eine Großstadt. Dieser Ort ist es auch, der als einziger in größerem Umfang „typisch Deutsches" vermitteln kann, das man in anderen Orten mit deutschem Namen vergeblich sucht. In der Architektur (z.B. Postamt, heute Museum) wie auch in der Kultur (Hermann-Denkmal oder Martin-Luther-College) sind deutsche Elemente noch heute deutlich sichtbar.

Sieht man von diesen Ansätzen - oder besser gesagt Relikten - des Deutschtums in Minnesota einmal ab, sind es allenfalls verwehte Spuren, die man bei genauerem Hinsehen da und dort noch entdecken kann. So ist Flensburg, Minnesota im Grunde eine polnische Siedlung, besser gesagt eine Siedlung von Amerikanern überwiegend polnischer Abstammung, deren Bewohner sich in keiner Weise mit dem deutschen Flensburg in Schleswig-Holstein identifizieren können, ja von dessen Existenz gar nichts wissen. Was für Flensburg gilt, mag für viele Orte im „Land des himmelfarbenen Wassers" zutreffen: Es sind historische Ortsgründungsnamen, fast ausschließlich aus dem 19. Jahrhundert. Ihre Gründer und Namensgeber ruhen längst auf den kleinen Pionierfriedhöfen. Ein Spaziergang durch dieselben ist gleichsam ein Gang durch die Vergangenheit. Schwerlich kann eine Siedlungsgeschichte besser kommentiert und dokumentiert werden als auf diesen Friedhöfen, die ein beredtes Zeugnis echten Pioniergeistes darstellen in einem Land, dem die Neuankömmlingen so fremd war, daß sie, egal ob aus Deutschland, Skandinavien oder Polen stammten, unwillkürlich auf einheimische Ortsbezeichnungen ihres Herkunftslandes zurückgriffen und sie so für alle Zeiten auf den Landkarten und Katasterbüchern verewigten. So gesehen sind die deutschen Ortsnamen in Minnesota nichts anderes als ein Hauch von Nostalgie, von Vergangenheit. Sie sind aber untrennbar mit der Besiedlungsgeschichte des Staates verbunden. Das gleiche gilt selbstverständlich auch für skandinavische, holländische, polnische oder südeuropäische Ortsbezeichnungen.

TYPOLOGY OF THE PLACE NAMES
Typologie der Ortsnamen

The German geographic names and place designations in Minnesota can be essentially classified into five categories:

1. Those place names which derive from German cities, e. g. Augsburg, Berlin, Bremen, Cologne (Köln) etc.

2. Those place names which go back to the names of German settlers, e. g. Besemann, Breitung, Buhl, Dassel, etc.

3. Those places which bear the names of important or legendary German personalities, e. g. Bismarck, Herman (The Cheruscan), Humboldt, Moltke, etc.

4. Those names which signify a German region, e. g. Franconia (Franken), Friesland, Krain, Nassau, North Germany (Norddeutschland), etc.

5. In addition there are those appelations which have either a purely geographic reference (e. g. Danube = Donau) or are of American origins (e. g. Custer = Küster). But even here the naming of places fits into our overall topic because they were conceived with reference to Germany, e. g. Germania, Germantown, Greenwald or Rheiderland.

Die deutschen geographischen Namen und Ortsbezeichnungen in Minnesota lassen sich im wesentlichen in fünf Gruppen einteilen:

1. Gruppe der Ortsnamen, die von deutschen Städten herrühren, z. B. Augsburg, Berlin, Bremen, Cologne (Köln), usw.

2. Gruppe der Ortsnamen, die auf deutsche Siedlernamen zurückgehen, z. B. Besemann, Breitung, Buhl, Dassel, usw.

3. Gruppe der Ortsnamen, die den Namen wichtiger oder legendärer deutscher Persönlichkeiten tragen, wie z. B. Bismarck, Hermann (der Cherusker), Humboldt, Moltke.

4. Gruppe der Ortsnamen, die deutsche Regionen repräsentieren, wie z. B. Franconia (Franken), Friesland, Krain, Nassau, North Germany (Norddeutschland), usw.

5. Daneben existieren Namensgebungen, die entweder rein geographischen (z. B. Danube = Donau) oder amerikanischen Ursprungs (z. B. Custer = Küster) sind. Aber auch Namensgebungen kommen vor, die zu diesem Zweck extra gebildet wurden, wie etwa Germania, Germantown, Greenwald oder Rheiderland.

DISTRIBUTION
Verteilung

German place names:

In total, there are 89 German place names which are distributed across 54 counties in Minnesota. We find them for cities, but also for small settlements and for townships. The concept of a "township" especially for the non-American reader, is in need of a brief explanation: A township is a typical North American measurement of land which was checkerboarded into originally six miles by six miles with 36 sections. The ideal township was formed also with six townships on a side so that there were theoretically 36 townships in each county. Seldom was this theory fully adhered to. Rather, the township and the counties were adjusted to reflect the cultural landscape with the result that the exact configuration varied somewhat from the theory. Each section was then further subdivided into quarter sections with 160 acres (65 hectares) each, which yielded the size of the customary homestead. Finally, each county was made up of townships which in some respect might reflect the population density.

German names are the most frequent for the designation of settlements and townships:

six times in St. Louis County,
five times in Stearns County,
four times each in Carver and Brown Counties,
three times each in Lyon, Chisago and Clay Counties.

German names for bodies of water:

It is no accident that Minnesota proudly calls itself the "land of 10,000 lakes", which is in actuality an understatement because far more than 12,000 have been ennumerated. Nowhere near all of them have names. Small lakes in out of the way territories even today are still officially nameless or bear names which are known only among the local people.

In the case of 162 bodies of water (lakes and streams) distributed across 44 counties, names of German origin were determined, among them:

seventeen in Otter Tail County,
fifteen in Carver County,
thirteen in Stearns County,
ten in St. Louis County,
eight each in Hennepin and Itasca Counties,
seven in Becker County,
six in Cook County,
five each in Brown and Crow Wing Counties,
four each in Douglas, Pine, Todd and Wright Counties.

German names for hills:

At least one hill in the otherwise rather flat state of Minnesota bears a German name. It is Ahrens Hill (Crow Wing County) and was named after the German immigrant farmer Charles (Karl) Ahrens.

Deutsche Siedlungsnamen:

Insgesamt 89 deutsche Ortsnamen verteilen sich auf 54 Counties (Landkreise) in Minnesota. Wir finden sie für Städte, aber auch für kleine Siedlungen und für Townships. Dabei bedarf der Begriff „Township" gerade für den nichtamerikanischen Leser einer kurzen Erläuterung: Eine Township ist eine für Nordamerika typische, schachbrettähnliche Landesaufteilungseinheit von ursprünglich sechs mal sechs Quadratmeilen mit 36 Sektionen zu je einer Quadratmeile. Sie bestimmt noch heute in großen Teilen der Staaten des Mittleren Westens die Kulturlandschaft, auch wenn sich Besitzeinheiten geändert haben mögen. Die Idealform einer Township war ursprünglich so ausgelegt, daß rein theoretisch 36 Townships eine County bildeten. Nur selten wurde jedoch diesem Idealbild entsprochen. Jede Sektion einer Township wurde überdies in Viertelsektionen zu je 160 acres (= 65 Hektar) aufgeteilt, dies entsprach der Größe eines Einödhofes. Schließlich wurde eine je nach Bevölkerungsdichte unterschiedlich große Anzahl von Townships zu einer **County** zusammengefaßt.

Am häufigsten sind deutsche Bezeichnungen für Siedlungen und Townships anzutreffen:

sechs mal in St. Louis County,
fünf mal in Stearns County,
je vier mal in Brown und Carver County,
je drei mal in Lyon, Chisago und Clay County.

Deutsche Gewässernamen:

Nicht umsonst nennt sich Minnesota stolz „Land der 10 000 Seen", wobei dies noch eine Untertreibung darstellt, denn es wurden weit mehr als 12 000 gezählt. Nicht alle tragen Namen, kleine Seen in entlegenen Gebieten sind noch heute offiziell namenlos bzw. tragen Namen, die nur lokal bekannt sind.

Bei 162 Gewässernamen (Seen und Flußläufe), verteilt auf 44 Counties, konnten deutsche Ursprünge festgestellt werden, davon

siebzehn in Otter Tail County,
fünfzehn in Carver County,
dreizehn in Stearns County,
zehn in St. Louis County,
je acht in Hennepin und Itasca County,
sieben in Becker County,
sechs in Cook County,
je fünf in Brown und Crow Wing County,
je vier in Douglas, Pine, Todd und Wright County.

Deutsche Bergnamen:

Mindestens eine Erhebung im ansonsten recht flachen Minnesota trägt nachweisbar einen deutschen Namen. Es ist dies der Ahrens Hill im Crow Wing County, benannt nach dem deutschen Auswandererfarmer Charles (Karl) Ahrens.

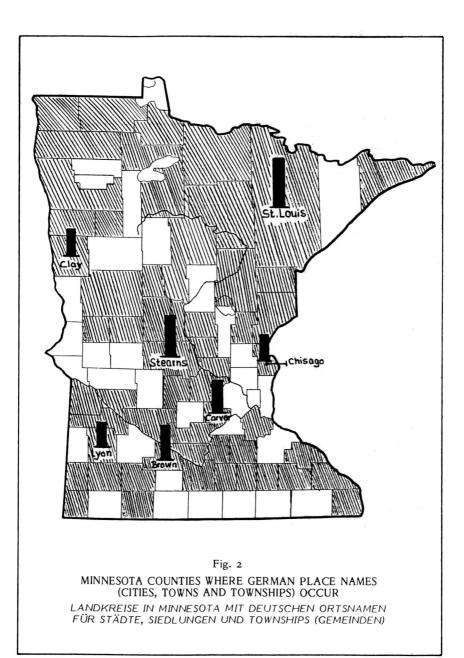

Fig. 2

MINNESOTA COUNTIES WHERE GERMAN PLACE NAMES
(CITIES, TOWNS AND TOWNSHIPS) OCCUR

*LANDKREISE IN MINNESOTA MIT DEUTSCHEN ORTSNAMEN
FÜR STÄDTE, SIEDLUNGEN UND TOWNSHIPS (GEMEINDEN)*

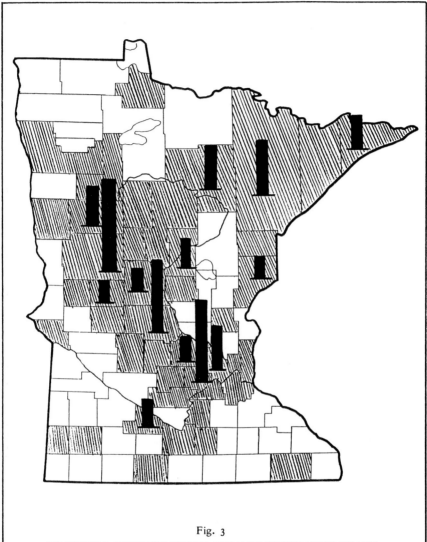

Fig. 3

MINNESOTA COUNTIES WHERE GERMAN GEOGRAPHIC NAMES
OF STREAMS AND LAKES OCCUR

*LANDKREISE IN MINNESOTA MIT DEUTSCHEN GEOGRAPHISCHEN
NAMENSBEZEICHNUNGEN FÜR GEWÄSSER*

OVERALL DISTRIBUTION
Gesamtverteilung

The total of 252 German geographic names referring to cities, villages, townships, bodies of water and hills occur in more than three quarters of all the counties of Minnesota. Put in another way, these geographic designations are distributed rather evenly across the entire state. Even a cursory glance at the map confirms this supposition. In central Minnesota, as a matter of fact, there is a chain of linked counties in which there is a concentration of German place designations (Carver, Stearns, Hennepin and Wright). At this point it is interesting to note that none of the counties bear German names.

The heaviest concentration of German names is in Carver County with nineteen geographic names, followed by Stearns and Otter Tail with eighteen each. In third place is St. Louis County in the upper regions of the state with sixteen German place names. Itasca, Brown, Cook, Hennepin and Becker counties each indicate more than half a dozen German names, interestingly enough, Hennepin and Becker having eight respectively seven geographic names for bodies of water but none for a town or a township. Counties without any German place names are mainly in the South and the West of Minnesota, but these are the minority as already indicated. In general it can be maintained that on the average, each county has three German place names.

In addition there are in the entire state more than two dozen geographic designations which sound German, and therefore could be of German origin. But these were not included in the list presented here because the possibility exists that they are either of Dutch or Scandinavian origin.

Die insgesamt 252 deutschen geographischen Namen, bezogen auf Städte, Dörfer, Townships, Gewässer und Erhebungen treten in mehr als drei Viertel aller Landkreise von Minnesota auf. Anders ausgedrückt: Diese geographischen Bezeichnungen verteilen sich ziemlich gleichmäßig über das ganze Staatsgebiet. Bereits ein flüchtiger Blick auf die Landkarte bestätigt diese Vermutung. Im zentralen Minnesota gibt es sogar eine zusammenhängende Kette von Landkreisen, in denen gehäuft deutsche Ortsbezeichnungen auftreten (Carver, Stearns, Hennepin und Wright). An dieser Stelle ist auch die Tatsache interessant, daß keiner der Landkreise einen deutschen Namen trägt.

Die größte Konzentration deutscher Ortsnamen finden wir in Carver County mit neunzehn Vorkommen, gefolgt von Stearns und Otter Tail mit je achtzehn. An dritter Stelle liegt St. Louis County im hohen Nordwesten mit sechzehn deutschen Namensgebungen. Die Landkreise Itasca, Brown, Cook, Hennepin und Becker weisen je etwas mehr als ein halbes Dutzend deutscher geographischer Namen auf; Hennepin County und Becker County interessanterweise acht beziehungsweise sieben geographische Namen für Gewässer, aber keinen für einen Ort. Landkreise ohne deutsche Ortsbezeichnungen kommen vor allem im Süden und Westen Minnesotas vor, sie sind aber, wie bereits oben angedeutet, stark in der Minderzahl. Generell kann gesagt werden, daß im Schnitt auf einen Minnesota-Landkreis drei deutsche Ortsnamen treffen.

Daneben gibt es im ganzen Staat mehr als zwei Dutzend geographische Bezeich-

Name einer ehemaligen Poststation in Milton (1858), benannt nach der Hauptstadt der Schweiz. Als Ortsname kommt er in Westdeutschland einmal vor (Nordrhein-Westfalen). Außerhalb Minnesotas gibt es je ein Bern in Indiana, Kansas, New York und Pennsylvanien; Alaska besitzt einen Ort namens New Bern (Neu-Bern).

BESEMANN   Carlton County
This township was named in honor of a former German landowner by the name of Ernest Besemann who later moved to Chaska in Carver County.
Die Township wurde nach einem deutschen Landeigentümer namens Ernst Besemann benannt, der später nach Chaska (Carver County) weiterzog.

BISMARCK   Sibley County
This township was settled in 1867 and named in honor of the great Prussian statesman, founder, and chancellor of the German empire, Otto Fürst von Bismarck-Schönhausen (1815-1898). Countless places in the United States bear this name, the most famous city being without doubt the capital of North Dakota. In West Germany a section of the city of Gelsenkirchen (North Rhine-Westphalia) bears this name. In the German Democratic Republic Bismark (without the 'c') occurs twice, once in the Altmark and again near Pasewalk.
Die Township wurde bereits 1867 besiedelt und von den ersten Bewohnern nach dem großen preußischen Staatsmann, Gründer und erstem Kanzler des Deutschen Reiches, Otto Fürst von Bismarck-Schönhausen, benannt (1815-1898). Zahlreiche Orte in den USA tragen diesen Namen, die bekannteste Stadt ist zweifelsohne die Hauptstadt Norddakotas. In Westdeutschland trägt ein Stadtteil von Gelsenkirchen (Nordrhein-Westfalen) diesen Namen; in der DDR kommt Bismark (ohne 'c') zweimal vor (in der Altmark und bei Pasewalk).

BREITUNG   St. Louis County
This township was named in honor of Edward Breitung who opened the Minnesota Mine, the first worked on the Vermilion Iron Range. Breitung was born in Schalkau (now the German Democratic Republic) and received his higher education in Meiningen (Thurinigia, German Democratic Republic).
Eine Township, die nach Edward (Eduard) Breitung benannt wurde, der die „Minnesota Mine", die erste in Betrieb genommene Mine auf der 'Vermilion Iron Range', eröffnete. Breitung stammte aus Schalkau (heute DDR) und erhielt seine Hochschulausbildung in Meiningen (Thüringen, heute DDR).

BREMEN   Pine County
The township was named by its first settlers who were from Germany and is identical with the large German port city on the North Sea in West Germany. Bremen occurs quite often in North America, e. g. in Alabama, Georgia, Indiana, Kansas, Kentucky, North Dakota and Ohio. As a place name in Germany it exists in two places in North Rhine-Westphalia as well as twice in Baden-Württemberg, and once in the German Democratic Republic.
Die Township wurde von ihren ersten Siedlern nach der gleichnamigen großen Hafenstadt in Westdeutschland benannt. Bremen kommt in Nordamerika mehrmals vor, z.B. in Alabama, Georgia, Indiana, Kansas, Kentucky, Norddakota und Ohio. Als Ortsname in Deutschland gibt es ihn je zweimal in Nordrhein-Westfalen und in Baden-Württemberg und einmal in der DDR.

BUHL (pop. 1303)   St. Louis County
So named in honor of the settler who was of German immigrant stock, Frank H. Buhl, the president of the Sharon Ore Company of Pennsylvania. Founded in 1901, Buhl is today an important iron mining center on the Mesabi Range.
Nach dem deutschstämmigen Auswanderer Frank H. Buhl benannt, Präsident der 'Sharon Ore Company' (Pennsylvanien). Heute ist Buhl, das 1901 gegründet wurde, ein bedeutender Bergbauort in der 'Mesabi Range' (Eisenerzabbau).

COBURG   Lyon County
Once this was the designation of a post office in Amiret township (1872), given in
honor of the first postmaster William Coburn. Quite likely this name occurs because of a misspelling. Coburg is a well-known county seat in Bavaria near the
border with the German Democratic Republic.
*Frühere Bezeichnung der Poststation in der Township Amiret (1872), benannt nach
dem ersten Postmeister, William Coburn. Vermutlich handelte es sich um eine
Falschschreibung. Coburg ist eine bekannte Kreisstadt in Bayern an der Grenze zur
DDR.*

COLOGNE (pop. 518)   Carver County
This railway village in Benton Township (incorporated 1881) was named by German
settlers for the large and ancient city of Cologne (Köln) on the Rhine. New Jersey
and Virginia likewise have a Cologne. The name itself derives from the Latin
"Colonia" (a settlement of Roman citizens in an occupied territory - e. g. 'Colonia
Agrippinensis' = Köln). In West Germany there is a Köln also in Bavaria.
*Die Eisenbahnsiedlung in der Benton Township (eingemeindet 1881) wurde von ihren
deutschen Siedlern nach der großen alten Stadt Köln am Rhein benannt. New Jersey und Virginia besitzen ebenfalls ein Cologne. Entstanden ist der Name aus dem
lateinischen "Colonia" (= Ansiedlung römischer Bürger in einem besetzten Gebiet,
z. B. 'Colonia Agrippinensis' = Köln). In Westdeutschland gibt es noch einen weiteren Ort mit dem Namen Köln (in Bayern).*

CUSTER   Lyon County
This township was settled in 1868 and organized in 1876. It was named in honor of
the famous George Armstrong Custer, a Major General of German origin who had
served in the American Civil War. His name originally was Küster. Custer was
born in Ohio in 1839 of parents who had come from Germany. Custer's fame derives from the "Battle on the Little Big Horn" in Montana where the Sioux Indians
massacred him and his regiment. In Colorado, Illinois, Kentucky, Michigan, Montana, Nebraska, Oklahoma, Pennsylvania, South Dakota, Washington and Wisconsin
there are places named after Custer.
*Die Township wurde 1868 besiedelt und nach dem berühmten George Armstrong
Custer, einem deutschstämmigen Generalmajor aus dem amerikanischen Bürgerkrieg, benannt. Hinter Custer verbirgt sich der deutsche Familienname Küster.
Custer wurde in Ohio geboren (1839), seine Eltern stammen aus Deutschland. Be-
rühmt wurde Custer durch die „Schlacht am Little Big Horn" in Montana, wo
Sioux-Indianer ihn und sein ganzes Regiment massakrierten. In Colorado, Illinois,
Kentucky, Michigan, Montana, Nebraska, Oklahoma, Pennsylvanien, Süddakota,
Washington und Wisconsin finden wir ebenfalls Orte mit dem Namen Custer.*

DANUBE (pop. 497)   Renville County
This is a railway village in Troy township, which was founded in 1899 and incorpo-
rated in 1901. The famous river in Europe after which it was named is the **Donau**.
It originates in Donaueschingen (Baden-Württemberg) and leaves Germany (Bavaria)
at Passau. After flowing a distance of 2,850 kilometers, it empties into the Black
Sea. The place name of Danube occurs likewise in the state of New York.
*Die Eisenbahnsiedlung in der Troy Township (gegründet 1899, eingemeindet 1901)
trägt den Namen eines berühmten europäischen Flusses: Donau. Sie entspringt in
Donaueschingen (Baden-Württemberg), verläßt bei Passau Bayern und mündet
schließlich nach 2850 km ins Schwarze Meer. Der Ortsname Danube kommt ebenfalls im Bundesstaat New York vor.*

DASSEL (pop. 1058)   Meeker County
Settlement in this township began in 1856 and ten years later was designated Swan
Lake. But in 1878 it was changed to honor the German settler Bernard Dassel who
had made a name for himself as secretary of the St. Paul and Pacific Railroad

Corporation. Dassel is also the name of a rather large city in Lower Saxony in West Germany.

Die Besiedlung dieser Township begann 1856 und erhielt zehn Jahre später den Namen Swan Lake; 1878 aber in die heutige Form umbenannt zu Ehren des deutschen Siedlers Bernard Dassel, der als Sekretär der St. Paul & Pacific Eisenbahngesellschaft sich einen Namen machte. Dassel ist auch der Name einer größeren Stadt in Niedersachsen.

DIETER   Roseau County
This township was named in honor of a German settler by the name of Martin Van Buren Dieter, who later moved to Montana.

Die Township wurde nach einem deutschen Siedler namens Martin Van Buren Dieter benannt, der später nach Montana verzog.

DRESBACH (pop. 120)   Winona County
This small village and township were founded in 1857 and named for George B. Dresbach who moved to this place from Ohio the same year and operated a farm and a stone quarry. Dresbach appears as a place name only once in West Germany, in the state of North Rhine-Westphalia.

Der kleine Ort und die Township wurden 1857 gegründet und nach George B. Dresbach benannt, der im gleichen Jahr aus Ohio hierher zog und eine Farm und einen Steinbruch betrieb. Dresbach kommt als Ortsname in Westdeutschland einmal (in Nordrhein-Westfalen) vor.

DUELM   Benton County
This small hamlet in section 34 of the county was named for the German settlers there. Benton County was one of the first counties organized in the Territory of Minnesota.

Der kleine Weiler in der Sektion 34 des Landkreises wurde nach seinen deutschen Siedlern benannt. Die Benton County war einer der ersten Landkreise, die im damaligen Minnesota-Territorium eingerichtet wurden.

EITZEN (pop. 208)   Houston County
The small village directly on the border with Iowa in the Winnebago district was given its name after the hometown of its first settler. The name occurs three times in West Germany, in Lower Saxony.

Das kleine Dorf, unmittelbar an der Grenze zu Iowa im Gebietsteil Winnebago gelegen, wurde nach dem Heimatort des ersten Siedlers benannt. Dieser Ortsname kommt in Westdeutschland dreimal vor (Niedersachsen).

ESSIG   Brown County
This small village in Milford township was named by C.C. Wheeler, a high official with the Chicago and Northwestern Railway to honor one of the Essig brothers who erected the first business structure in this region. The man's name was John Essig, an Illinois farmer who came to Minnesota with his parents in 1866. His father, John F. Essig, was born in Germany. In Germany this name to designate a place comes up once in North Rhine-Westphalia and once in Bavaria.

Der kleine Ort in der Milford Township wurde von C.C. Wheeler, einem hohen Beamten der Chicago & Northwestern Railway so benannt, um einen der Gebrüder Essig zu ehren, der das erste Geschäftsgebäude in dieser Gegend errichtete. Es handelte sich um John Essig,einen Farmer aus Illinois, der mit seinen Eltern 1866 nach Minnesota kam. Sein Vater, John F. Essig, war gebürtiger Deutscher. In Deutschland kommt der Name als Ortsbezeichnung je einmal in Nordrhein-Westfalen und in Bayern vor.

FELDMAN   Koochiching County
This township in northern Minnesota got its name from the first settler here, Feldmann, a well-known German family name. Feldman township was established relatively late, in 1916.

Diese Township im nördlichen Minnesota erhielt ihren Namen nach einem der ersten Siedler, Feldmann, einem gebräuchlichen deutschen Familiennamen. Feldman Township wurde erst relativ spät, 1916, eingerichtet.

FLENSBURG (pop. 259)   Morrison County
This small railway village, platted in 1890, was named for the seaport and fjord in Schleswig-Holstein.
Die kleine Eisenbahnsiedlung (1890 entstanden), erhielt ihren Namen nach der Stadt Flensburg in Schleswig-Holstein an der gleichnamigen Förde (Bucht).

FRANCONIA   Chisago County
Founded in 1858 and officially recorded in 1884, this township got its name from Ansel Smith, the first settler in the region, who came from Franconia, New Hampshire. Franconia is the Latin name for a region (Franken) in Bavaria. In the United States there is a place by the name of Franconia also in Virginia and in Pennsylvania. Frankenmuth is in Michigan.
Die Township, 1858 gegründet und 1884 amtlich eingetragen, erhielt ihren Namen von Ansel Smith, dem ersten Siedler der Region, der aus Franconia, New Hampshire, stammte. Franconia ist die lateinische Bezeichnung für eine bayerische Region (Franken). Als Ortsname ist Franken einmal in Rheinland-Pfalz und zweimal in Bayern vertreten. In den Vereinigten Staaten gibt es je einen Ort Franconia in Virginia und in Pennsylvanien. Frankenmuth ist eine Ortschaft in Michigan.

FRANKFORT   Wright County
This township was first settled in 1854. The majority of the German settlers decided on the name Frankfurt which was, then as now, one of the major cities in Germany. Later the name was anglicized to Frankfort. This place name occurs frequently in North America, though sometimes with the final letter 'd', e. g. in Delaware, Illinois, Indiana, Kansas, West Virginia, and Ontario, Canada. In addition to Frankfurt on the Main River, and a village by the same name in Bavaria, there is also Frankfurt on the Oder River in the German Democratic Republic.
Die Township wurde 1854 erstmals besiedelt. Die Mehrzahl der deutschen Siedler entschied sich für den Namen Frankfurt, damals wie heute eine der bedeutendsten Städte in Deutschland. Aus Frankfurt wurde später das amerikanische Frankfort. Dieser Ortsname, öfters auch mit einem 'd' am Schluß geschrieben, kommt in Nordamerika häufig vor, so unter anderem in Delaware, Illinois, Indiana, Kansas, Kentucky, Maine, Michigan, Missouri, New York, Ohio, Pennsylvanien, Süddakota, West Virginia und Ontario (Kanada). Neben Frankfurt am Main und einem gleichnamigen Dorf in Bayern gibt es noch ein Frankfurt an der Oder (DDR).

FREDENBERG   St. Louis County
This township was named in honor of Jacob Fredenberg, one of its German pioneer settlers.
Die Township wurde nach einem ihrer ersten Siedler, dem Deutschen Jacob Fredenberg, benannt.

FREEBURG   Houston County
This first settlement in Crooked Creek township got its name from the first settlers who had come from Freiburg im Breisgau (Baden-Württemberg). Two towns in Lower Saxony likewise bear this name. In an anglicized American form it is rather frequent in America, e. g. Fryeburg in Maine and Fryburg in North Dakota. There is also a settlement with the German spelling in Ontario, Canada.
Die kleine Siedlung in der Crooked Creek Township erhielt ihren Namen von den ersten Ansiedlern, die aus Freiburg im Breisgau (Baden-Württemberg) stammten. Zwei Orte in Niedersachsen tragen ebenfalls diesen Namen. In amerikanisierter Form ist Freiburg öfters in Amerika vertreten, z. B. als Fryeburg in Maine und Fryburg in Norddakota. Außerdem gibt es ein Freiburg (deutsche Schreibung) in Ontario (Kanada).

FRIBERG   Otter Tail County
This township was established on January 6, 1874 and at first called Florence, later Woodland. On June 1, 1874 it was re-titled with its present name in honor of
settlers from the region of Freiberg in Saxony (today the German Democratic Republic). In the GDR there is a second town by the same name in the vicinity of
Adorf in the Vogtland. In West Germany Friberg is the place name of five towns,
four in Bavaria and one in Baden-Württemberg.
*Die Township wurde am 6. Januar 1881 eingerichtet und zunächst Florence, später
Woodland genannt. Am 1. Juni 1874 erhielt sie ihren jetzigen Namen von Siedlern,
die aus der Gegend von Freiberg in Sachsen (heute DDR) stammten. In Mitteldeutschland gibt es noch einen weiteren Ort gleichen Namens in der Gegend von
Adorf im Vogtland. In Westdeutschland ist Freiberg als Ortsname fünfmal
vertreten (viermal in Bayern, einmal in Baden-Württemberg).*

FRIESLAND   Pine County
This train station five miles north of Hinckley very likely received its name from
the north German region called Friesland, that is the region between the rivers
Rhine and Weser. Administratively Friesland today is a county in the state of
Lower Saxony. Moreover, a district of Holland also bears this name so that the
possibility exists - though it is not likely - that the name was brought to Minnesota by Dutch settlers. As a place name, Friesland occurs in Germany twice in
Lower Saxony. In Wisconsin, there is also a town called Friesland while in Michigan there is a Vriesland.
*Die Bahnstation fünf Meilen nördlich von Hinckley erhielt ihren Namen höchst-
wahrscheinlich von Siedlern aus dem historischen Friesland in Norddeutschland,
dem Gebiet zwischen den Flüssen Rhein und Weser. Verwaltungsmäßig gesehen ist
Friesland heute ein Landkreis in Niedersachsen. Eine holländische Provinz trägt
übrigens den gleichen Namen, so daß es möglich, aber wenig wahrscheinlich ist,
daß der Name von holländischen Siedlern nach Minnesota getragen wurde. Als
Ortsname kommt Friesland in Deutschland zweimal in Niedersachsen vor. In Wisconsin, USA, trägt ein Ort den gleichen Namen, in Michigan gibt es ein Vriesland.*

FULDA (pop. 1226)   Murray County
This small town in southwestern Minnesota got its name from its first settlers in
honor of their hometown, Fulda in the state of Hesse, a city with a very famous
cathedral in whose crypt since 744 has lain the grave of St. Boniface, the patron
saint of the Germans. It lies on a river of the same name. The name Fulda is
somewhat well known as a place name in North America, occurring at least in
Saskatchewan, Canada and Indiana where settlements were named in its honor.
*Das Städtchen im Südwesten Minnesotas erhielt seinen Namen von seinen ersten
Siedlern nach deren Heimat Fulda in Hessen, einer deutschen Stadt mit bedeutendem Dom (alte Krypta von 744 mit Grab des hl. Bonifatius), am gleichnamigen
Fluß gelegen. Fulda ist als Ortsname in Nordamerika nicht unbekannt, in Saskat-
chewan (Kanada) und in Indiana gibt es Siedlungen dieses Namens.*

GERMANIA   Todd County
It can be assumed that the name of this township which was established in 1880
was suggested by Paul Steinbach who had come to America on the vessel "Germania". As a place name, Germania is known also in Pennsylvania, Virginia and Wisconsin. In West Germany there is a small village in North Rhine-Westphalia which
likewise bears this name.
*Man nimmt an, daß der Name der Township (1880 gegründet) vom deutschen Sied-
ler Paul Steinbach vorgeschlagen wurde, der mit dem Schiff „Germania" nach
Amerika kam. Germania ist als Ortsname in Amerika unter anderem in Pennsylvanien, Virginia und Wisconsin noch erhalten. In Westdeutschland gibt es ein kleines
Dorf in Nordrhein-Westfalen, das ebenfalls diesen Namen trägt.*

GERMANTOWN   Cottonwood County
This place which originated in 1874 received its name from the many German
settlers there, who were in the majority in that southwestern Minnesota region at
the time. Germantown is common in America, being in use at least in Illinois,
Kentucky, Maryland, New York, North Carolina, Ohio, Pennsylvania, Tennessee and
Wisconsin.
*Dieser Ort, 1874 entstanden, erhielt seinen Namen von den vielen deutschen Sied-
lern, die damals, zu Beginn der Besiedlung dieses südwestlichen Teils von Minnesota, zahlenmäßig weit in der Überzahl waren. Germantown gibt es viele in Amerika, so unter anderem in Illinois, Kentucky, Maryland, New York, Nordkarolina,
Ohio, Pennsylvanien, Tennessee und Wisconsin.*

GOTHA   Carver County
This small hamlet in Hancock township was named for the settlers from a city of
the same name in Thuringia in central Germany, today in the German Democratic
Republic. In the GDR there is a second town by that name near Eilenburg. In West
Germany there is no place called Gotha.
*Der kleine Weiler in der Gemeinde Hancock wurde von den ersten Einwanderern
nach der gleichnamigen mitteldeutschen Stadt in Thüringen (heute DDR) benannt.
In der DDR gibt es noch einen weiteren Ortsnamen Gotha bei Eilenburg; in West-
deutschland kommt dieser Name nicht vor.*

GREENWALD (pop. 244)   Stearns County
This name in Grove Township is half English and half German. Obviously behind its
present spelling is the German 'Grünwald', meaning in English 'Green Grove'. This
appellation occurs once in Baden-Württemberg and three times in Bavaria. Grünwald is also a municipal subdivison of the city of Munich.
*Der Ort in Grove Township trägt einen zur Hälfte englischen, zur Hälfte deut-
schen Namen. Unschwer verbirgt sich dahinter der deutsche Ortsname Grünwald,
der einmal in Baden-Württemberg und dreimal in Bayern vorkommt. 'Wald' bedeutet im Englischen 'grove'. Grünwald ist außerdem ein Stadtteil von München.*

HACKENSACK (pop. 220)   Cass County
Hackensack was a railway village between Brainerd and Bemidji named for an earlier post-office which derives from the town of Hackensack in New Jersey on the
river by the same name, which name was given to it by James Curo, the first
postmaster, ranchman and merchant there. It is not clear where the German name
actually comes from. It is not known as a place name in Germany, however, there
are many places with the first two syllables 'Hacken", such as Hackenbach,
Hackenberg, Hackendorf, Hackenheim and others.
*James Curo, der erste Postmeister, Rancher und Händler in dieser Gegend, nannte
diese ehemalige Eisenbahnsiedlung zwischen Brainerd und Bemidji nach einer frü-
heren Poststation, deren Name von dem gleichnamigen Ort in New Jersey am
Hackensack River herrührt. Es ist nicht geklärt, woher der deutschklingende Name
kommt; als Ortsname ist er in Deutschland unbekannt, jedoch gibt es viele Orte
mit der Anfangssilbe 'Hacken-' wie Hackenbach, Hackenberg, Hackendorf, Hackenheim, usw.*

HADLER   Norman County
A small railway settlement in Pleasant View Township which was titled after the
first settler, Jakob Hadler, who from 1909 until 1915 was a member of the board
of county commissioners.
*Kleine Eisenbahnsiedlung in der Pleasant View Township, die nach dem ersten
Siedler, Jakob Hadler, benannt wurde, der von 1909 bis 1915 dem Rat der Bevoll-
mächtigten des Landkreises Norman angehörte.*

HAGEN   Clay County
This township was named after either the first settler in the region (a Norwegian

or a German), or perhaps after the large city with the same name in the state of North Rhine-Westphalia in West Germany. This name, however, also occurs at least 40 times elsewhere in West Germany; and in the German Democratic Republic there is also a town on the Island of Rügen by the name of Hagen. In North America the name is also used for a town in the Canadian province of Saskatchewan.

Die Township wurde entweder nach dem ersten Siedler in dieser Gegend, einem Norweger (oder Deutschen) oder nach der gleichnamigen Großstadt in Nordrhein-Westfalen benannt. Der Ortsname kommt in Westdeutschland insgesamt vierzig mal vor; in der DDR gibt es auf der Insel Rügen einen Ort namens Hagen. In Nordamerika finden wir diesen Ortsnamen in der kanadischen Provinz Saskatchewan wieder.

HAMBURG (pop. 377)   Carver County

The first German settlers here named their railroad station in honor of the largest German harbor city on the Elbe. With its 1.6 million inhabitants, it is the second largest city in all of West Germany. In North America Hamburg occurs also in Arkansas, California, Connecticut, Illinois, Iowa, Louisiana, Michigan, Mississippi, Missouri, New Jersey, New York, Pennsylvania and Wisconsin. In Ohio and Illinois, there are two names of Hamburg, in Canadian Ontario, in Missouri, New York and Pennsylvania there is also a New Hamburg. Hamberg in North Dakota is probably a misspelling of the same name. Surprisingly, in all of Germany there is only one other small village (in North Rhine-Westphalia) by the name of Hamburg.

Die ersten deutschen Siedler benannten diese Eisenbahnstation nach dem größten deutschen Seehafen an der Elbe (mit 1,6 Millionen Einwohnern die zweitgrößte Stadt Westdeutschlands). In Nordamerika tragen viele Orte den Namen Hamburg; so gibt es je ein Hamburg in Arkansas, Kalifornien, Connecticut, Illinois, Iowa, Louisiana, Michigan, Mississippi, Missouri, New Jersey, New York, Pennsylvanien und Wisconsin. In Ohio und Illinois kommt Hamburg gleich zweimal vor, im kanadischen Ontario gibt es, ebenso wie in Missouri, New York und Pennsylvanien, je ein New Hamburg. Hamberg in Norddakota könnte auf eine falsche Schreibweise zurückgeführt werden. Interessanterweise gibt es in ganz Deutschland neben dem großen Hamburg nur noch ein kleines Dorf in Nordrhein-Westfalen, das ebenfalls diesen Namen trägt.

HANOVER (pop. 365)   Wright County

The small town of Hanover on the Crow River in Minnesota is a peculiar place: It is situated in a township which likewise has a famous German name: Frankfort. The founders were two brothers with the surname of Vollbrecht (1877), who named the place in honor of their city of birth. The place name 'Hanover' (nearly always written with only one 'n') is among the most frequent names for German settlements in North America (along with Hamburg, Berlin, and Bremen). It also occurs in Arkansas, Connecticut, Illinois, Indiana, Kansas, Maine, Maryland, Michigan, Montana, New Hampshire, New Mexico, North Dakota, Ohio, Pennsylvania, Virginia, West Virginia, Wisconsin and Ontario, Canada. In Massachusetts there is a North, a South and a West Hanover in addition to a Hanover Center. In Pennsylvania there is Hanoverdale and Hanover Junction. In Virginia we find Hanovertown and Hanover Junction. In North Carolina there is a New Hanover. As a place name Hanover occurs only once in all of Germany, namely as the capital city of Lower Saxony.

Kurios verhält es sich mit dem kleinen Ort Hanover am Crow River in Minnesota: Er liegt in einer Township, die ebenfalls einen deutschen Namen trägt: Frankfort. Als Gründer zeichnen die Gebrüder Vollbrecht (1877), die diesem Ort zu Ehren ihrer Geburtsstadt diesen Namen gaben. Der Ortsname Hanover (fast immer nur mit einem 'n' geschrieben) kommt neben Hamburg, Berlin und Bremen am häufigsten in deutschen Siedlungsgründungen in Nordamerika vor; wir finden ihn unter anderem in Arkansas, Connecticut, Illinois, Indiana, Kansas, Maine, Maryland, Michigan, Montana, New Hampshire, New Mexico, Norddakota, Ohio, Pennsylvanien, Virginia, West Virginia, Wisconsin und Ontario (Kanada); in Massachusetts gibt es ein North, South und West Hanover, ebenso ein Hanover Center; in Pennsylvanien ein Hanoverdale und Hanover Junction; in Virginia Hanovertown und Hanover Junction; in Nordkarolina ein New Hanover. Als Ortsname kommt Hannover in ganz Deutschland nur einmal vor, nämlich als Hauptstadt Niedersachsens.

HAMMER   Yellow Medicine County
The township was settled beginning in 1872 primarily by newcomers from Bavaria and Prussia. In West Germany there are 27 places called Hammer, and in the German Democratic Republic two, a name that usually implies the word in German 'Hammerwerk', a hammer mill. In Tennessee there is also a town by the name of Hammer.

Die Township wurde ab 1872 vornehmlich von bayerischen und preußischen Einwanderern besiedelt. 27 Orte in Westdeutschland und zwei Orte in Mitteldeutschland (heute DDR) tragen diesen Namen, der in den meisten Fällen auf ein Hammerwerk hinweist. In Tennessee gibt es ebenfalls einen Ort namens Hammer.

HEIDELBERG   Le Sueur County
The settlers arrived from southwestern Germany and poured into this region in the 1870s. They named this small town after the famous university city on the Neckar River in Baden-Württemberg. Heidelberg is one of the most beautifully situated of German cities and is home to the oldest university on German soil (1386). The city remained untouched by the Second World War. As a place name Heidelberg occurs only one more time in West Germany (in Hesse). It is used also in Kentucky, Mississippi, Missouri, Pennsylvania, and in Ontario, Canada.

Die Siedler aus Südwestdeutschland, die ab den 70er Jahren des letzten Jahrhunderts in diese Gegend einströmten, benannten den kleinen Ort nach der bekannten Universitätsstadt am Neckar in Baden-Württemberg. Heidelberg ist eine der schönstgelegenen deutschen Städte und besitzt die älteste Universität auf deutschem Boden (1386). Sie blieb im 2. Weltkrieg gänzlich unzerstört. Als Ortsname kommt Heidelberg nur noch einmal in Westdeutschland vor (in Hessen). In Kentucky, Mississippi, Missouri, Pennsylvanien und Ontario (Kanada) stoßen wir ebenfalls auf diesen Ortsnamen.

HERMAN (pop. 619)   Grant County
This railway village in Logan township was platted in 1875. In 1914 it was selected by the State Municipality League as a "model town" on account of its civic merit. The name was given by high railroad officials in honor of Hermann Trott, a land agent of the St. Paul and Pacific, who was born in Hannover, Germany and died in St. Paul in 1903. The place name "Hermann" does not exist as such in Germany but in the United States it is known in Michigan and Missouri and with two n's, and in Nebraska and Pennsylvania with one. Quite likely the name usage in the United States derives from the famous Hermann the Cheruscan, a General of the Germanic tribes in Roman times, who has been in the United States by the lodges that were founded under his name. He stands in the form of an immense statue in the Teutoburger Forest in Germany, and on the Heights overlooking the city of New Ulm in Minnesota.

1914 wurde der Ort (1875 angelegt) zur „Modellstadt Minnesotas" auserkoren. Hohe Eisenbahnbeamte verliehen der Bahnsiedlung ihren Namen, der an Hermann Trott erinnern soll, damals Grundstücksmakler der St. Paul & Pacific Eisenbahngesellschaft. Hermann Trott wurde 1830 in Hannover (Deutschland) geboren und starb 1903 in St. Paul (Minnesota). Den Ortsnamen „Hermann" gibt es in dieser Form in Deutschland nicht; in den Vereinigten Staaten kommt er dagegen in Michigan, Missouri (mit zwei 'n'), Nebraska und Pennsylvanien vor. Mit hoher Wahrscheinlichkeit

*wird die Namensgebung in den Vereinigten Staaten mit dem berühmten Cherusker-
fürsten der germanischen Stämme in der Römerzeit in Verbindung gebracht, der in
Form einer riesigen Statue im Teutoburger Wald zu sehen ist und dessen amerika-
nisches Pendant auf einer Anhöhe das Minnesotastädtchen New Ulm überblickt.*

HERMANTOWN (pop. 6737)   St. Louis County
This suburb of Duluth was at first called Herman, so titled in honor of Hermann
the Cheruscan (17 B.C. - 21 A.D.), for his defeat of the Romans in the Teutoburger Forest in 9 A.D. Hermann was originally called Arminius in the Latin version
of his name. He is honored as the liberator of the German people from the Roman
yoke. A Hermannstadt does not exist in Germany, but in the Siebenbürgen region
of Romania there is a city by this name which was founded by German emigrants
to that region. It served as the capital city of the region from the 12th to the
19th centuries. The Romanian name today is written Sibiu.
*Dieser Vorort von Duluth hieß früher Herman, benannt von seinen deutschen Sied-
lern nach Hermann dem Cherusker (17 v.Chr. bis 21 n.Chr.), dem berühmten
Helden aus der Schlacht gegen die Römer im Teutoburger Wald (9 n.Chr.). Hermann (eigentlich Arminius) gilt als der „Befreier Germaniens". Eine Ortsgründung
mit dem Namen Hermannstadt existiert in Deutschland nicht, aber in Rumänien
(Siebenbürgen) gründeten im 12. Jahrhundert deutsche Auswanderer ein Hermanns-
dorf, das als Hermannstadt vom 12. bis 19. Jahrhundert die Hauptstadt Siebenbür-
gens war. Der heutige rumänische Name ist Sibiu.*

HIBBING (pop. 16104)   St. Louis County
This largest mining city on the Mesabi Range got its name from its founder, Frank
Hibbing. He was born in 1857 in Germany and came to the United States as a boy
with his parents. He is credited with discovering the Hibbing ore beds in 1892, the
largest in all of North America. Frank Hibbing died in Duluth in 1897.
*Die größte Bergbaustadt in der 'Mesabi Range' erhielt ihren Namen nach ihrem
Gründer, Frank Hibbing. Er wurde 1857 in Deutschland geboren und kam als Junge
mit seinen Eltern nach Amerika und entdeckte 1892 die riesigen Eisenerzvorkom-
men im Norden Minnesotas. Frank Hibbing starb 1897 in Duluth.*

HOFFMAN (pop. 627)   Grant County
A railway village in Land Township which reveived its name from Robert C. Hoffmann of Minneapolis, who, for many years, had been chief engineer of the Minneapolis, St. Paul and Sault Ste. Marie Railway. Hoffmann is one of the most widely
used German surnames. As a place name, it is also common in the United States
(e. g. Oklahoma). In Germany it never occurs as a place name, although there is a
town in Bavaria by the name of Hofmanns.
*Die Eisenbahnsiedlung in der Land Township erhielt ihren Namen von Robert C.
Hoffmann, der viele Jahre lang Oberlokführer der 'Minneapolis, St. Paul & Sault
Ste. Marie Eisenbahn' war. Hoffmann ist einer der bekanntesten deutschen
Familiennamen. Als Ortsname ist er in den USA nicht unbekannt (z. B. in Oklahoma). In Deutschland tritt er als Ortsname nicht in Erscheinung, lediglich in Bayern
gibt es eine Ortschaft Hofmanns.*

HUMBOLDT   Clay County
This township was settled by a German colony and named in honor of the celebra-
ted German scientist, traveler, and author, Alexander von Humboldt (1769 - 1859).
In the years 1799 - 1804 Humboldt traveled in South America and Mexico, and later published many books on his observations of the natural sciences, history and
political affairs on this continent. As a place name in Germany, Humboldt occurs
only once (as a section of the city of Köln on the Rhine) while in the New World
this name for towns is extremely prominent, e. g. in Arizona, South Dakota,
California, Illinois, Iowa, Kansas, Michigan, Nebraska, Ohio, Pennsylvania and
Tennessee. A county in Nevada also bears this name.

Die Township wurde von deutschen Kolonisten besiedelt, die den Namen in Erinnerung an den großen deutschen Wissenschaftler und Reiseautor Alexander von
Humboldt (1769 - 1859) für dieses Gebiet auswählten. Humboldt bereiste von 1799
bis 1804 große Teile Süd- und Mittelamerikas und veröffentlichte später eine
ganze Reihe von Büchern über seine naturwissenschaftlichen und historisch-politi-
schen Reisebeobachtungen. Als Ortsname tritt Humboldt in Deutschland nur einmal
(als Stadtteil von Köln am Rhein) in Erscheinung, während in der „Neuen Welt"
dieser Ortsname äußerst geläufig ist (z.B. in Arizona, Kalifornien, Illinois, Iowa,
Kansas, Michigan, Nebraska, Ohio, Pennsylvanien, Süddakota und Tennessee). Ein
Landkreis in Nevada trägt ebenfalls diesen Namen.

HUMBOLDT (pop. 112) — Kittson County

This small town in the southeastern part of St. Vincent Township was likewise
named after the famous German scientist Baron Alexander von Humboldt. Kittson
County is the northwesternmost county in Minnesota. The town of Humboldt itself
lies only ten miles south of the Canadian border.

Die kleine Ortschaft im südöstlichen Teil der St. Vincent Township wurde ebenfalls
nach dem großen deutschen Wissenschaftler Baron Alexander von Humboldt
benannt. Kittson County ist der nordwestlichste Landkreis Minnesotas; der Ort
Humboldt selbst liegt nur 10 Meilen südlich der kanadischen Grenze.

IHLEN (pop. 132) — Pipestone County

A small village in Eden Township received its name from the first settler there,
the German Carl (Karl) Ihlen (1888).

Das kleine Dorf in der Township Eden erhielt seinen Namen nach dem ersten Siedler, dem Deutschen Carl (Karl) Ihlen (1888).

KEIL — Beltrami County

This township was probably named in honor of a German settler. Keil means "wed-
ge" in English. As a place name in Germany there is one occurence in Lower Saxony. There is also the possibility that this is a misspelling for Kiel, the capital
city of Schleswig-Holstein in northern Germany.

Die Township wurde wahrscheinlich nach einem deutschen Siedler benannt. Als
Ortsname kommt er in Deutschland einmal vor (Bezeichnung eines Dorfes in Niedersachsen). Möglich ist auch eine Falschschreibung und der Name lautete ursprünglich Kiel, die Hauptstadt von Schleswig-Holstein.

KLOSSNER (pop. 90) — Nicollet County

A settlement in Lafayette Township named after a Swiss German Jakob Klossner
who was born in Switzerland in 1846 and came to the United States at the age of
three with his parents. The family moved to Minnesota in 1856. He served, in order to contain the uprising of the Sioux, with the the Minnesota Mounted Rangers
from 1862-63. He owned a farm near New Ulm and was a representative in the
legislature in 1878.

Eine Siedlung in der Township Lafayette, benannt nach dem Schweizerdeutschen
Jakob Klossner, der 1846 in der Schweiz zur Welt kam und im Alter von drei Jahren mit seinen Eltern in die Vereinigten Staaten übersiedelte. Nach Minnesota zog
die Familie im Jahre 1856. Im Sioux-Aufstand 1862-63 diente Klossner bei den
„Minnesota Mounted Rangers", einer berittenen Spezialeinheit. Er besaß eine Farm
in der Nähe von New Ulm und war Abgeordneter in der gesetzgebenden Versammlung (1878).

KONIG — Beltrami/Lake of the Woods County

The township was named in honor of a German settler and undoubtedly was originally written "König". The name occurs once in Germany in the form of Bad König (Hesse).

Die Township erhielt ihren Namen nach einem deutschen Siedler, der höchstwahr-
scheinlich ursprünglich König hieß. Als Ortsname gibt es ihn in Deutschland einmal

in Form von Bad König (Hessen).

KOST   Chisago County
This small settlement in southern Sunrise Township received its name from Ferdinand A. Kost who built a grain mill there in 1883.
Die kleine Ansiedlung im südlichen Teil der Township Sunrise erhielt ihren Namen von Ferdinand A. Kost, der 1883 hier eine Getreidemühle errichtete.

KRAIN   Stearns County
This township, which was organized about 1868, received its name from the territory belonging formerly to Austria-Hungary (Slovenia). From this region came Father Francis Xavier Pirec (Pierz), who is credited among other things with the founding of St. John's College and Abbey. Pierz was also responsible for recruiting hundreds of German colonists for Stearns and Benton Counties. He also gave his name to a city in the latter.
Die Township, die ab 1868 entstand, erhielt ihren Namen von einem Gebiet im ehemaligen Österreich-Ungarn (Slowenien). Aus dieser Gegend stammte auch Reverend Francis Xavier Pirec (oder Pierz), dem man unter anderem die Gründung des St. John's College nebst Abtei zuschreibt. Pirec (Pierz) war es auch, der deutschstämmige Kolonisten zu Hunderten nach Stearns County und Umgebung brachte. Ein Städtchen erhielt sogar seinen Namen.

KROSCHEL   Kanabec County
A township that received its name from a settler called Hermann Kroschel.
Die Township erhielt ihren Namen nach dem Siedler Hermann Kroschel.

KUGLER   St. Louis County
This township was named after Fred (Fritz) Kugler who was one of the county commissioners. As a place name it occurs once in Bavaria.
Die Township wurde nach Fred (Fritz) Kugler benannt, der dem Kommittee der Landkreisbevollmächtigten im St. Louis County angehörte. Als Ortsname kommt Kugler einmal in Bayern vor.

KURTZ   Clay County
Named in honor of Thomas C. Kurtz, the son of Colonel John D. Kurtz, who was highly decorated in the Civil War. Kurtz or Kurz is a common German surname.
Benannt nach Thomas C. Kurtz, dem Sohn von Oberst John D. Kurtz, der im amerikanischen Bürgerkrieg hoch dekoriert wurde. Kurtz oder Kurz ist ein gebräuchlicher deutscher Familienname.

LUTSEN (pop. 250)   Cook County
Hidden behind the Americanized spelling is the name of the German city Lützen, which lies southwest of Leipzig in Saxony, today the German Democratic Republic, and is well known in history on account of the Battle at Lützen (1632) where King Gustavus Adolphus of Sweden fell in battle.
Hinter dieser amerikanisierten Schreibweise verbirgt sich die Stadt Lützen südwestlich von Leipzig (Sachsen, heute DDR), bekannt geworden durch die „Schlacht bei Lützen" (1632), wo König Gustav Adolf von Schweden fiel.

MANFRED   Lac qui parle County
This township which was settled in 1876, was first given the name of Custer in honor of the famous General George A. Custer. But in 1884 the name was changed to Manfred to honor the principle character in a wild and weird dramatic poem by Lord Byron, the English Romantic poet who lived for ten years in Switzerland and wrote this poem with its Alpine setting. Manfred is a common German first name. A town in North Dakota bears the same name.
Die Township (1876 besiedelt), wurde zunächst mit dem Namen Custer versehen zu Ehren des berühmten Generals George A. Custer (Küster). 1884 änderte man die Bezeichnung der Township in Manfred um. Manfred ist die Hauptfigur in einem

Gedicht von Lord Byron (englischer Dichter der Romantik, der zehn Jahre in der Schweiz lebte und dieses Gedicht in der Alpenwelt ansiedelte). Manfred ist im übrigen ein gebräuchlicher deutscher Vorname. Ein Ort in Norddakota trägt den gleichen Namen.

METZ Wadena County

This was a post office in the township of North Germany. German settlers wanted to commemorate the city in Lorraine which was German from 1870 until 1918, and from 1940 till 1945. Metz is also a common German family name, especially in South Germany. As a place name it occurs three times with the suffix '-dorf', that is as Metzdorf in West Germany and once in the German Democratic Republic.

Name einer ehemaligen Poststation in der Township North Germany. Deutsche Siedler wollten damit eine Erinnerung an die Stadt in Lothringen schaffen, die von 1870 bis 1918 und 1940 bis 1945 deutsch war. Metz ist ebenfalls ein gebräuchlicher deutscher Familienname, vor allem in Süddeutschland. Als Ortsname tritt er dreimal in Verbindung mit '-dorf' (Metzdorf) in Westdeutschland und einmal in der DDR auf.

MILLERSBURG Rice County

A village in Forest Township, platted in 1857 by George W. Miller (undoubtedly Müller).

Ein Dorf in der Township Forest, das 1857 von George W. Miller angelegt wurde. Hinter diesem amerikanisierten Namen versteckt sich zweifellos der ursprüngliche Name Müller.

MILLERVILLE (pop. 109) Douglas County

Established as a township in 1867 and incorporated as a village in 1903, this town takes its name from John Miller, the Americanized version of Hans Müller. Müller is one of the most common German surnames.

Name einer Township (gegründet 1967) und eines Ortes (1903 amtlich eingetragen) nach einem der ersten Siedler, John Miller (dem amerikanisierten Hans Müller). Müller gehört zu den häufigsten deutschen Familiennamen.

MINDEN Benton County

Undoubtedly the township was titled after the city of the same name in Westphalia. There is a second Minden in West Germany in Bitburg County (Rhineland-Palatinate). As a place name, Minden is used frequently in North America — in Iowa, Louisiana, Nevada, Texas, West Virginia and Ontario, Canada. Over and above these, there is a Minden City in Michigan, and in Missouri we find Minden Mines while in Illinois there is a New Minden.

Sicherlich wurde die Township nach der gleichnamigen Stadt in Westfalen benannt. Es gibt aber in Westdeutschland noch ein weiteres Minden im Kreis Bitburg (Rheinland-Pfalz). Als Ortsname ist Minden in Nordamerika stark vertreten; wir treffen ihn in Iowa, Louisiana, Nevada, Texas, West Virginia und Ontario (Kanada) an. Darüber hinaus gibt es in Michigan eine Minden City, in Missouri die Minden Mines und in Illinois ein New Minden.

MOLTKE Sibley County

The German settlers in the area wanted to honor the Prussian Field Marshal Helmut Count von Moltke (1800 - 1891) who was victorious in the wars of 1866 and 1870-71. Moreover, Moltke was a significant military writer. The township of Moltke was organized relatively late (1875). In West Germany there is no place name Moltke, although there is a Moltkestein in Schleswig-Holstein.

Die deutschen Siedler ehrten mit dieser Namensgebung den preußischen Generalfeldmarschall Helmut Graf von Moltke (1800 - 1891), der die siegreichen Kriege von 1866 und 1870/71 leitete. Daneben war Moltke ein bedeutender Militärschrift-

steller. Die Township Moltke wurde erst relativ spät besiedelt (1875). In West-
deutschland gibt es keinen Ortsnamen Moltke, lediglich ein Moltkestein (in Schles-
wig-Holstein).

NASSAU (pop. 126)   Lac qui parle County
This village was organized as a railway settlement in 1893 and received its name
from settlers who titled it in honor of the former German duchy (since 1906, formerly just a county), which was named after the fortress of Nassau on the Lahn
River. The settlers wanted to preserve the name in the New World. A city on the
Lahn in the Rhineland-Palatinate also bears this name. Two other places in Baden-
Württemberg and in Bavaria are also called by this name. In the German Democratic Republic, too, there is a Nassau. In North America Nassau is used in at
least three states, Delaware, Florida, and New York. Nassau is also the capital
city of the Bahamas.
Der Ort wurde als Eisenbahnsiedlung 1893 gegründet und erhielt seinen Namen von
Siedlern, die die Bezeichnung der ehemaligen Grafschaft (ab 1806 Herzogtum, be-
nannt nach der Burg Nassau an der Lahn) in der Neuen Welt lebendig erhalten
wollten. Auch eine Stadt an der Lahn in Rheinland-Pfalz trägt diesen Namen, zwei
weitere Orte in Baden-Württemberg und in Bayern heißen ebenso. Auch in der
DDR gibt es ein Nassau. In Nordamerika kommt Nassau als Ortsbezeichnung in
mindestens drei Bundesstaaten vor (Delware, Florida und New York). Nassau heißt
auch die Hauptstadt der Bahamas.

NESSEL   Chisago County
Named in honor of the earliest pioneer farmer in the region, Robert Nessel, who
was born in Germany in 1834, and came with his parents to the United States in
1847, and to Minnesota in 1854 where he settled two years later in the place to
which he gave his name.
Benannt nach dem frühesten Pionierfarmer in dieser Gegend, Robert Nessel, der
1834 in Deutschland zur Welt kam, 1847 mit seinen Eltern in die Vereinigten Staa-
ten auswanderte und 1854 nach Minnesota gelangte, wo er sich zwei Jahre später
an dem nach ihm benannten Ort niederließ.

NEW GERMANY (pop. 303)   Carver County
This small town started as a typical railway settlement in the Midwest and re-
ceived its name in honor of the many German immigrants in the vicinity. During
World War I its name was changed to Motordale, in order to exhibit the displeasu-
re of the state officials with Germany, but was subsequently re-titled with its original designation. There is a New Germany in Ohio and in Nova Scotia, Canada.
Das kleine Landstädtchen entstand als typische Eisenbahnsiedlung des Mittleren
Westens und erhielt den Namen zu Ehren der vielen deutschen Einwanderer in der
Umgebung. Während des 1. Weltkrieges taufte man den Ort in Motordale um, was
den Unmut gegenüber Deutschland in dieser Zeit zum Ausdruck bringen sollte. Je
ein New Germany gibt es noch in Ohio und Neuschottland (Kanada).

NEW MUNICH (pop. 307)   Stearns County
This small town in Oak Township is situated near Interstate 94. It began as a
postal station. This community in which nearly everyone has a German name is
deeply Catholic. The huge church is dedicated to the Immaculate Conception,
modelled in a way after the Church of our Lady ('Frauenkirche') in Munich. A Bavarian settler to the region named it in honor of his state capital, which after
Berlin and Hamburg holds title to being the third largest city in all of Germany.
The place name München occurs three more times in Germany - in the Upper Palatinate, in Lower Bavaria and in the German Democratic Republic near Weimar.
As a place name in the United States we find it also in North Dakota.
Das Landstädtchen in der Township Oak unweit der Schnellstraße 'Interstate 94'
war zunächst nur eine kleine Poststation. Der kleine Ort ist streng katholisch, die

meisten Einwohner tragen noch deutsche Familiennamen. Die monumentale Kirche „Zur unbefleckten Empfängnis" paßt so gar nicht in das Ortsbild. Als Vorlage dien-te die Münchner Marienkirche (Frauenkirche). Ein bayerischer Siedler war es auch, der zu Ehren der bayerischen Landeshauptstadt (nach Berlin und Hamburg dritt-größte westdeutsche Stadt) diese Namensgebung vornahm. Der Ortsname München kommt in Deutschland noch dreimal vor: In der Oberpfalz, in Niederbayern und in der DDR (bei Weimar). Als amerikanischen Ortsnamen treffen wir ihn in Norddakota an (Munich).

NEW TRIER (pop. 153)   Dakota County
Several settlers from the Rhineland-Palatinate named this town after their home-land, the well-known city on the Moselle, which began as a Roman colony.
Einige Siedler aus Rheinland-Pfalz nannten diese Siedlungsstelle nach ihrer Hei-mat, der bekannten Stadt an der Mosel, die als römische Kolonie Augusta Trevero-rum um 15 v. Chr. von Kaiser Augustus gegründet wurde.

NEW ULM (pop. 13051)   Brown County
This county seat on the Minnesota River is no doubt the best known and the largest city in Minnesota that bears a German place name. In 1854-55 German colonists comprised of workers from Chicago and Cincinnati (the so-called 'Tur-nerbund' - a more or less socialistic society) arrived in the vicinity of present day New Ulm. Since 20 of the first 32 settlers originated from the town of Ebrach in Württemberg not far from the city of Ulm, they called the settlement 'Ulm' in honor of this large city on the Danube. In 1862 New Ulm was completely de-stroyed by an Indian uprising, an event that has gone down in history as the "New Ulm Massacre". Many inhabitants were killed. The court martial perpetrated by the whites was bitter: in the neighboring city of Mankato on December 26, 1862, the largest Indian sentencing in US history took place when 38 Indians were hanged. The Sioux uprising is commemorated in New Ulm today with a "Defender's Monu-ment".
Incorporated as a town in 1857 and as a city in 1876, the city received its present charter in 1887. The pioneer spirit of the 19th century can still be felt in this most German of all settlements in Minnesota. In scarcely any other city in the United States is the German spirit - at least nominally - so present as in New Ulm. This is especially true in the local business world where German family na-mes still play an important role. The monument to Hermann represents the Ger-man spirit, a somewhat accurate reproduction of the original in the Teutoburger Forest. The "Glockenspiel" or clock tower with musical carillon in the downtown area with its 37 bells and figures reminds visitors of the "Schäfflertanz" on the Munich City Hall. Dr. Martin Luther College and Domeier's German Store (a shop with German retail sales - a unique concept in the United States) remind one of the contemporary German mentality.
In a cultural vein, the German spirit is kept alive in New Ulm by "Faschingsfest" in the winter and the "Heritage Fest" in summer. The singing society "Concord Singers" is famous far beyond the borders of Minnesota.
The German sister city and university town of Ulm on the Danube in Baden-Würt-temberg nourishes its contacts with the American city of New Ulm. The German Ulm appears in documents as early as 854. In its famous cathedral which was con-structed between 1377 and 1533, the city possesses the highest church tower on earth (162 meters). On the opposite bank of the Danube River lies the Bavarian city of Neu-Ulm, a good sized industrial city. Interestingly, there is another place name of Ulm in Baden-Württemberg and yet another by this name in the state of Hesse.
The name Ulm occurs four times in the United States. New Ulm in Austin County, Texas (650 inhabitants), which was founded by German settlers, is a few years older than New Ulm in Minnesota. In Arkansas there is a farming community

called Ulm with 150 inhabitants, and an Ulm in both Wyoming and Montana.

Der Landkreissitz am Minnesota River ist zweifelsohne die bekannteste und größte Stadt in Minnesota, die einen deutschen Ortsnamen trägt. 1854-55 kamen deutsche Kolonisten, organisierte Arbeiter aus Chicago und Cincinnati (der sog. „Turnerbund", eine mehr oder weniger sozialistische Vereinigung) in die Gegend des heutigen New Ulm. Da zwanzig der ersten zweiunddreißig Siedler ursprünglich aus dem württembergischen Ebrach unweit von Ulm stammten, gab man der kleinen Siedlung den Namen nach der großen Stadt an der Donau, Ulm. New Ulm wurde 1862 beim großen Indianeraufstand völlig dem Erdboden gleichgemacht (in die Geschichte als „das Massaker von New Ulm" eingegangen), viele der Einwohner wurden getötet. Das Strafgericht der Weißen war grausam: Im nahegelegenen Mankato wurden am 26. Dezember 1862 38 Indianer in der größten Massenhinrichtung der Vereinigten Staaten gehenkt. An den Sioux-Aufstand erinnert in New Ulm noch das „Defenders' Monument".

1876 bzw. 1887 erhielt New Ulm die Stadtrechte. Der Pioniergeist des 19. Jahrhunderts ist in der deutschesten aller Siedlungen in Minnesota noch gegenwärtig. In kaum einer weiteren Stadt in den Vereinigten Staaten ist das Deutschtum - zumindest dem Namen nach - noch so gegenwärtig. Das trifft vor allem auf die Geschäftswelt zu, wo deutsche Familiennamen immer noch eine dominierende Rolle spielen. Typisch Deutsches repräsentiert das Hermann-Denkmal, eine getreue Nachbildung des gleichnamigen Originals im Teutoburger Wald; das „Glockenspiel", ein Musikturm im Zentrum der Stadt mit 37 Glocken und Figuren, die stark an den Schäfflertanz am Münchner Rathaus erinnern, ist ebenso zu nennen wie das Dr. Martin-Luther-College und Domeier's German Store (ein Kaufladen mit deutschen Waren, der in dieser Form wohl einmalig in den ganzen USA sein dürfte).

Kulturell wird das Deutschtum in New Ulm durch das Faschingsfest im Winter und das Heritagefest (Erbgutfest) im Sommer hochgehalten. Die Gesangsgruppe „The Concord Singers" ist weit über Minnesota hinaus bekannt.

Die deutsche Paten- und Universitätsstadt Ulm an der Donau in Baden-Württemberg pflegt traditionell seit langem Kontakte mit dem amerikanischen New Ulm. Das deutsche Ulm wird bereits 854 erstmals urkundlich erwähnt. Mit dem bekannten Münster (1377 - 1533 erbaut) besitzt es den höchsten Kirchturm der Erde (162 m). Gegenüber von Ulm, nur durch die Donau getrennt, liegt das bayerische Neu-Ulm, eine bedeutende Industriestadt. Interessanterweise gibt es sowohl in Baden-Württemberg wie auch in Hessen je einen weiteren Ortsnamen Ulm.

Viermal kommt dieser Ortsname noch in den Vereinigten Staaten vor. New Ulm im Austin County von Texas (650 Einwohner) wurde 1847 von deutschen Siedlern gegründet, ist also um ein paar Jahre älter als New Ulm in Minnesota. In Arkansas gibt es eine Farmgemeinde Ulm (150 Einwohner), je ein Ulm treffen wir noch in Wyoming und in Montana an.

NORTH GERMANY   Wadena County

This township reveived its name from the first German colonist to the area, probably from the North German area. The German translation 'Norddeutschland' signifies the region covered roughly by the states of Lower Saxony, Schleswig-Holstein, Hamburg and Bremen.

Die Township erhielt von ihren ersten Kolonisten (wohl aus dem norddeutschen Raum stammend) ihren Namen. Die deutsche Übersetzung 'Norddeutschland' bezeichnet geographisch die Bundesländer Niedersachsen, Schleswig-Holstein, Hamburg und Bremen.

PIERZ (pop. 893)   Morrison County

The township and later the settlement was named in honor of the Catholic missionary Francis Xavier Pierz, born an Austrian from the German-speaking language island of Krain, today in Yugoslavia. Between 1852 and 1873 he did missionary work among the Objibwa Indians in Minnesota. He is responsible also for the influx

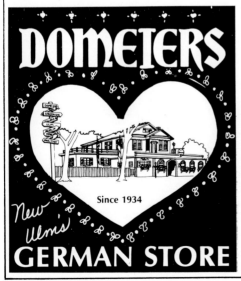

of German settlers to the counties of Stearns and Morrison. In 1873 he returned to Austria and died in the city of Laibach, the former capital city of the crown territory, Krain, known today as Lublijana (Slovenia), Yugoslavia. The town by the name of Pierz was platted in 1891, and incorporated in 1892. The railway settlement of New Pierz immediately to the south, which originated in 1908, was retitled Genola.

Benannt wurde die Township und spätere Siedlung nach dem katholischen Missionar Francis (Franz) Xavier (Xaver) Pierz (Pirec), einem gebürtigen Österreicher aus der deutschen Sprachinsel Krain (heute Jugoslawien), der zwischen 1852 und 1873 Missionsarbeit bei den Objibwa-Indianern in Minnesota betrieb. Er zeichnete auch für den Zustrom von deutschen Siedlern in den Landkreisen Stearns und Morrison verantwortlich. 1873 kehrte er nach Österreich zurück und verstarb 1880 in Laibach (ehemaliges österreichisches Kronland Krain, heute Lublijana, Slowenien/Jugoslawien). 1891-92 entstand die nach ihm benannte Siedlung Pierz. Die Eisenbahnsiedlung New Pierz unmittelbar südlich davon (1908 entstanden) wurde 1915 in Genola umbenannt.

POSEN   Yellow Medicine County
Settled beginning in 1868, this township received its name through German settlers from the former Prussian province of Posen (a province lying between the Oder and Weichsel Rivers in current day Poland). The city of Posen (today in Polnish Poznán) is a very old bishopric with a historical cathedral dating from 1433. In the current day German Democratic Republic there is also a place name Posen. This name occurs in the United States, furthermore, in Illinois.

Die Township, ab 1868 besiedelt, erhielt ihren Namen von deutschen Siedlern aus der ehemaligen preußischen Provinz Posen (zwischen Oder und Neiße, heute Polen). Die Stadt Posen (heute polnisch Poznán) ist ein uralter Bischofssitz mit bedeutendem Dom (1433 begonnen). In der heutigen DDR gibt es ebenfalls noch den Ortsnamen Posen. In den Vereinigten Staaten taucht diese Bezeichnung in Illinois nochmals auf.

POTSDAM   Olmsted County
This small settlement in the township of Farmington was founded by colonists from Prussia in 1860, who wanted to commemorate this neighboring city of Berlin which lies on the Havel River. It is less than 50 miles east of a township in Steele County by the name of Berlin. Potsdam is today a major city in the German Democratic Republic. Potsdam is also known as the high-class secondary (summer) residence of the Brandenburg-Prussian rulers, with many palaces and beautiful parks. It is also famous as the site of the Potsdam Conference held in July, 1945 and the Potsdam Treaty that followed it on August 8, 1945. Potsdam is also the name of a small village in Schleswig-Holstein. In the United States we find the name also in New York and Ohio.

Die kleine Siedlung in der Township Farmington wurde von preußischen Kolonisten um 1860 gegründet, die mit dieser Namensgebung die Nachbarstadt von Berlin, an der Havel gelegen, ehren wollten. Potsdam, Minnesota liegt weniger als 50 Meilen östlich einer Township im Landkreis Steele, die den Namen Berlin trägt! Heute ist das originale Potsdam eine bedeutende Stadt in der DDR. Bekannt wurde sie als brandenburgisch-preußische Residenz (neben Berlin) mit Schloß und vielen herrlichen Parks und durch das „Potsdamer Abkommen" und die „Potsdamer Konferenz" (Juli/August 1945). Potsdam heißt auch ein kleiner Ort in Schleswig-Holstein. In den Vereinigten Staaten finden wir diese Ortsbezeichnung in den Bundesstaaten New York und Ohio vor.

RHEIDERLAND   Chippewa County
This township was established in 1887 and might have been named by settlers from the city of Rheydt (today a section of the city of Mönchengladbach). Two other places, to be sure with the spelling of Rheidt, also exist in the state of North

Rhine-Westphalia.
Die Township wurde 1887 eingerichtet und dürfte von nordrheinischen Siedlern nach der Stadt Rheydt (heute ein Stadtteil von Mönchengladbach) benannt worden sein. Zwei Orte, allerdings Rheidt geschrieben, finden wir ebenfalls noch in Nordrhein-Westfalen vor.

RHINEHART   Polk County
Although the actual name came from Captain A. C. Rhinehart from East Grand Forks who was a member of the county commissioners, there lies at the core of this Americanized name the common German name of Reinhard.
Die Township erinnert mit ihrem Namen an Hauptmann A. C. Rhinehart aus East Grand Forks, der ein Mitglied des Kommittees der Landkreisbeauftragten war. Hinter diesem amerikanisierten Namen ist unschwer der deutsche Vorname Reinhard erkennbar.

ST. AUGUSTA (pop. 200)   Stearns County
Founded in 1854, this township was first called Berlin, later Neenah, and in 1863 the name of the first church which was built here in 1856 by Father Francis Pierz was adopted. The village of St. Augusta came about as a way station on the Great Northern Railroad.
Die Township wurde 1854 besiedelt und zuerst Berlin, später Neenah genannt. 1863 erhielt sie von Vater Franz Pierz nach der ersten Kirche auf diesem Platz (1856 erbaut) den jetzigen Namen. Der Ort St. Augusta entstand 1855 an der 'Great Northern Railroad'-Eisenbahnstrecke.

ST. WENDEL   Stearns County
Settled following 1854, this township was called Hancock in the spring of 1868 and in the summer of the same year changed to St. Wendel. The name suggests German origins, for St. Wendel is a well-known city in the Saarland.
Die Township wurde ab 1854 besiedelt, im Frühjahr 1868 in Hancock umbenannt und im Sommer des gleichen Jahres wieder in St. Wendel umgetauft. Der Name läßt auf eine deutsche Gründung schließen; St. Wendel ist eine bekannte Stadt im Saarland.

SCHNEIDER LAKE   Mahnomen County
Within the borders of a township by the same name is a lake which supplied the name for the general region. The German Frank Schneider lived on this lake, was married to an Indian woman of the Ojibwa tribe and farmed in the area. Later he moved to Waubun in the same district. There are place names of 'Schneider' also in Scott and Polk counties. The name means 'tailor' in English and occurs twice in Germany, once in Baden-Württemberg and once in Bavaria. The name also occurs in the state of Indiana.
Innerhalb der Grenzen dieser Township liegt der gleichnamige See, der dem ganzen Landkreis seinen Namen gab. An besagtem See lebte der Deutsche Frank Schneider, der mit einer Indianerfrau aus dem Stamme der Ojibwa(y) verheiratet war, als Farmer. Später verzog er nach Waubun (im gleichen Distrikt). Der Ortsname Schneider kommt in Deutschland zweimal vor (in Baden-Württemberg und in Bayern). Im amerikanischen Bundesstaat Indiana gibt es ebenfalls einen Ort namens Schneider.

SCHROEDER (pop. 400)   Cook County
This settlement which has the same name as the township was titled after the president of a lumbering corporation in Ashland and Milwaukee, Wisconsin, John Schroeder. Schroeder is a family name that commonly occurs in northern Germany. There is one town in Texas by the name of Schroeder but as a place name it is unknown in Germany.
Die Siedlung in der gleichnamigen Township wurde nach dem Präsidenten einer Holzgesellschaft in Ashland und Milwaukee (Wisconsin), John Schroeder, benannt.

Schröder ist ein in Nord- und Westdeutschland häufig anzutreffender Familienname. In Texas heißt ein Ort ebenfalls Schroeder, in Deutschland ist diese Ortsbezeichnung unbekannt.

SIGEL   Brown County

Settled beginning in 1856, this township was named in honor of a Civil War general Franz Sigel. He was born 1824 in Sinsheim (Baden-Württemberg) and died in New York in 1902. In 1852 he arrived in the United States, settled in St. Louis as a teacher at a German school (1858), and recruited a regiment of volunteers in 1861, becoming its colonel. Sigel thereafter had rapid success in his military career and reached the rank of a general. With this rank, he visited the city of New Ulm in 1873 and saw the township which as yet had no name. Sigel is used also as a place name in Pennsylvania.

Die Township, ab 1856 besiedelt, wurde nach einem General im Bürgerkrieg, Franz Sigel, benannt, der 1824 in Sinsheim (Baden-Württemberg) zur Welt kam und 1902 in New York verstarb. 1852 kam er in die Vereinigten Staaten, siedelte sich in St. Louis als Lehrer an einem deutschen Institut an (1858) und richtete ein Regiment mit Freiwilligen ein (1861), dem er als Oberst vorstand. Sigel hatte in der Folgezeit eine steile militärische Karriere und erreichte den Rang eines Generals. Als solcher besuchte er auch um 1873 die Stadt New Ulm und die Township, die nach ihm benannt wurde. Als Ortsname kommt Sigel in den USA nochmals in Pennsylvanien vor.

STARK   Brown County

Following initial settlement in 1858, this township received the name of a German pioneer farmer, August Starck. The name here is not to be confused with the town of the same name in Chisago County, where Stark's origins go back to a Swedish family name. As a place name Stark occurs also in the state of Kansas.

Die Township wurde ab 1858 besiedelt und nach dem deutschen Pionierfarmer August Starck benannt. Nicht verwechselt werden darf die Township im Landkreis Brown mit dem gleichnamigen Ort Stark in Chisago County, der schwedischen Ursprungs ist. Stark ist sowohl ein deutscher wie schwedischer Familienname. Als Ortsnamen treffen wir ihn in den Vereinigten Staaten nochmals im Bundesstaat Kansas an.

THEILMAN   Wabasha County

A railway station in the southwest part of West Albany township, this name goes back to Henry (Heinrich) Theilmann, which doubtless is of German origins.

Die Eisenbahnsiedlung im südwestlichen Teil der Township West Albany wurde nach Henry (Heinrich) Theilmann benannt. Der Familienname ist zweifellos deutschen Ursprungs.

UNDINE REGION   Blue Earth County

Joseph N. Nicollet, one of the great explorers of Minnesota during the 19th century, on an 1841 map of the area of Blue Earth County, sketched in the concept of 'Undine Region' for the adjacent territory running eastward from the Redwood River to the Cannon River and from the Minnesota River southwards to the northern border of Iowa. Undine, the female water sprite, who had no soul, lived on in the forests and rivers of southern Minnesota, according to Nicollet. Quite likely Nicollet was inspired by the German writer, Friedrich Heinrich Karl de la Motte Fouqué (1777 - 1843). Fouqué was a poet in the German Romantic school who originated in Prussian Brandenburg. His prose fairy tale "Undine" was published in 1811.

Joseph N. Nicollet, einer der großen Erforscher Minnesotas im 19. Jahrhundert, verzeichnete auf einer Karte von 1841 die Gegend des heutigen Blue Earth County und deren Umgebung mit dem Begriff „Undine Region", die sich vom Redwood River östlich zum Oberlauf des Cannon River und vom Minnesota River südwärts bis zur Nordgrenze von Iowa erstreckte. Nicollet verpflanzte die germanische Undine-Sage in den Mittleren Westen Amerikas. Undine, der weibliche Wassergeist, der keine Seele besitzt, lebte nach Nicollet in den Wäldern und Flüssen Süd-Minnesotas fort. Zweifellos wurde Nicollet von Friedrich Heinrich Karl de la Motte Fouqué (1777 - 1843) inspiriert, einem deutschen Dichter der jüngeren Romantik, der aus dem preußischen Brandenburg stammte. Sein Prosamärchen „Undine" wurde 1811 publiziert.

VIENNA   Rock County
A township organized in 1874 which got its name from D. A. Hart in whose house the first township meeting was held. With the name is called in mind the capital city and cultural center of the Austrian empire, the numerous world-famous buildings such as the Cathedral of St. Stephen, the Habsburg administrative offices (Hofburg) and the Schönbrunn (summer palace), among others. Therefore the name appears in numerous settings in the United States, among them in Georgia, Illinois, Louisiana, Maine, Maryland, Michigan, Missouri, New Jersey, New York, Ohio, South Dakota, Virginia, West Virginia and Wisconsin. Likewise, a town in Ontario, Canada bears this name. In Ohio there is also a New Vienna.
Die Township wurde 1874 eingerichtet und bekam ihren Namen von D. A. Hart, in dessen Haus die erste Versammlung abgehalten wurde. Hinter dem Namen verbirgt sich die Hauptstadt und der kulturelle Mittelpunkt Österreichs mit den zahlreichen weltberühmten Bauten wie Stephansdom, Hofburg und Schloß Schönbrunn. Als Ortsname kommt Wien in Westdeutschland nur noch einmal vor (bei Inzell in Bayern). Die Ortsbezeichnung ist dagegen in zahlreichen Bundesstaaten der USA anzutreffen, so u. a. in Georgia, Illinois, Louisiana, Maine, Maryland, Michigan, Missouri, New Jersey, New York, Ohio, Süddakota, Virginia, West Virginia und Wisconsin. Ebenso trägt ein Ort in Ontario (Kanada) diesen Namen. In Ohio gibt es noch ein New Vienna.

WAGNER   Aitkin County
This township was named in honor of Bessie Wagner. Wagner is a well-known German family name. As a place name it appears also in Baden-Württemberg. In the United States it appears in California, Montana, and South Dakota.
Die Township wurde nach einer Frau namens Bessie Wagner benannt. Wagner ist ein bekannter deutscher Familienname. Als Ortsname kommt er einmal in Baden-Württemberg vor. In den USA stoßen wir in Kalifornien, Montana und Süddakota auf diese Ortsbezeichnung.

WALDORF   Waseca County
This small village in Vivian Township was named after a settlement in Maryland. The second syllable '-dorf' is a German word and means in English 'village'. In Germany there are hundreds of places with '-dorf' as a suffix. The special name Waldorf occurs three times in Germany, twice in North Rhine-Westphalia and once in Rhineland-Palatinate.
Der kleine Ort in der Township Vivian wurde nach einer Siedlung in Maryland benannt. Die zweite Silbe, '-dorf', ist ein deutsches Wort und bedeutet im Englischen 'village'. In Deutschland gibt es Hunderte von Ortsnamen, die auf '-dorf' enden. Der spezielle Ortsname Waldorf kommt dreimal in Deutschland vor, zweimal in Nordrhein-Westfalen und einmal in Rheinland-Pfalz.

WEIMER   Jackson County
This place was first called Eden when organized in 1871. But in the same year it was re-titled to its present name, which, in spite of its erroneous spelling, recalls the German city of Weimar. The first settler in the township was Charles (Karl) Winzer who chose the name to honor his home town in Saxony-Weimar. This well known city in Thuringia (today German Democratic Republic) was in Goethe's time the center of German culture (Goethe, Schiller, Herder, Wieland and others).

The concept "Weimarer Republik" was coined in this city. In California and Texas there are also towns by the name of Weimar.

Der Ort, 1871 entstanden, wurde zunächst Eden benannt. Noch im gleichen Jahr taufte man ihn in den jetzigen Namen um, der eine Falschschreibung des deutschen Ortsnamens Weimar darstellt. Der erste Siedler in der Township, Charles (Karl) Winzer, wählte diesen Namen zu Ehren seiner Heimatstadt in Sachsen-Weimar. Die bekannte Stadt in Thüringen (heute DDR) war zu Goethes Zeiten ein Zentrum des deutschen Geisteslebens (Goethe, Schiller, Herder, Wieland, und andere). Der Begriff „Weimarer Republik" wurde durch diese Stadt geprägt. In Kalifornien und in Texas gibt es ebenfalls je ein Weimar.

WESTERHEIM   Lyon County
Although of Norwegian origins, this name means "home in the west", which is also a German place name, occurring twice in Germany, once in Baden-Württemberg and once in Bavaria.

Der Name ist zwar norwegischen Ursprungs und bedeutet so viel wie „westliches Heim" oder „Westheim", er ist aber zugleich ein deutscher Ortsname, der zweimal in Westdeutschland auftritt (in Baden-Württemberg und in Bayern).

WIRT   Itasca County
This township was named by O. E. Walley for the first settler, probably for a township in New York, possibly Virginia, where the name honors William Wirt (1772 - 1834), the attorney general of the United States from 1817 - 1829. 'Wirt' is the German word for innkeeper and is relatively unknown as a family name, and if so, then with an 'h' at the end of the name. It means also 'landlord', 'host', but as a place name is unknown in Germany.

Die Township wurde von ihrem ersten Siedler, O. E. Walley, wahrscheinlich nach dem gleichnamigen Ortsnamen in New York bzw. Virginia benannt, wo man dieselben zu Ehren des Oberstaatsanwalts William Wirt (1772 - 1834) bezeichnete. Wirt ist ein relativ unbekannter deutscher Familienname, der meist am Schluß mit einem 'h' geschrieben wird. Als Ortsname ist er in Deutschland unbekannt.

ZIMMERMAN (pop. 495)   Sherburne County
This place in the township of Livonia was titled to honor a German-American farmer by the name of Zimmermann. Previously the place was called Lake Fremont. This customary German family name in English means "carpenter". As a place name it occurs in Germany only once, in Baden-Württemberg. In Louisiana the name exists in its original German spelling with double 'n'.

Der Ort in der Township Livonia wurde nach einem deutschstämmigen Farmer namens Zimmermann benannt (vorher hieß der Ort Lake Fremont). Der gebräuchliche deutsche Familienname Zimmermann bedeutet im Englischen „carpenter". Als Ortsname kommt er in Deutschland einmal vor (in Baden-Württemberg). In Louisiana, USA, gibt es einen weiteren Ort namens Zimmermann (diesmal mit der richtigen deutschen Schreibweise: 'nn' am Schluß).

ZIPPEL   Lake of the Woods County
A township which received its name in honor of a German by the name of William M. Zippel, who for a long time earned his living as a fisherman on Lake of the Woods. Zippel Creek which flows into this lake, earlier received its name from the same individual.

Die Township erhielt ihren Namen nach einem Deutschen namens William M. Zippel, der lange Zeit als Fischer am Lake of the Woods seinen Lebensunterhalt verdiente. Ein Bach, der in diesen See mündet, erhielt bereits früher von der gleichen Person seinen Namen (Zippel Creek).

BODIES OF WATER
Gewässer

ACHMAN LAKE   Stearns County

ALDERMATT LAKE   Brown County
Named for a Swiss farmer in Leavenworth Township, by the name of Hans B. Aldermatt.
In der Township Leavenworth gelegen, benannt nach dem Schweizer Farmer Hans B. Aldermatt.

AMBERGER LAKE   Lake County

BACHMAN LAKE   Carver County

BAUMBACH LAKE   Douglas County
Named in honor of Frederick von Baumbach who was born in Prussia in 1838 and died in Alexandria, Minnesota in 1917. He came to the United States in 1848 with his father, served in several different regiments during the war and then settled in 1867 in Alexandria where he held various positions, for example as secretary of state from 1880 - 1887.
Benannt zu Ehren von Frederick von Baumbach, 1838 in Preußen geboren und 1917 in Alexandria, Minnesota, verstorben. In die Vereingten Staaten kam er 1848 mit seinem Vater, diente in verschiedenen Regimentern und siedelte sich 1867 in Alexandria an und bekleidete mehrere hochrangige Posten, z. B. die eines Staatssekretärs (1880 - 1887).

BAVARIA LAKE   Carver County
So called in honor of the land of origin of the first settlers, namely, Bavaria.
Benannt nach dem Ursprungsland der ersten Siedler in dieser Gegend, nämlich Bayern.

BERLINER LAKE   Carver County
Named for a settler from Berlin, it is situated in Section 12 of Camden Township.
In Sektion 12 der Township Camden gelegen; benannt nach einem Siedler aus Berlin.

BOEDIGHEIMER LAKE   Otter Tail County

BURAN'S LAKE   Carver County
Named in honor of a farmer from Germany who settled in the area.
Benannt nach einem deutschstämmigen Farmer, der sich in der Nähe niederließ.

DOERFLER LAKE   Wright County

FISCHER LAKE   Scott County

FLANDRAU CREEK   Pipestone County
Today this is sometimes written as Flandreau Creek. But it was named after Charles Eugene Flandrau who was born in New York in 1828 and died in St. Paul, Minnesota in 1903. He was one of the more influential personalities in Minnesota in the 19th century. Judge Flandrau in 1862 commanded the volunteers against the Sioux Indians. Many other names go back to Flandrau, for instance a park near New Ulm, the above mentioned creek and others bearing this name of German origin, but which have mostly been transcribed later to bear a French sounding

spelling.

Meist Flandreau Creek geschrieben; benannt nach Charles Eugene Flandrau (geboren 1828 in New York, gestorben 1903 in St. Paul, Minnesota). Flandrau war wohl eine der bekanntesten Persönlichkeiten im Minnesota des 19. Jahrhunderts. Richter Flandrau kommandierte 1862 das Freiwilligenheer gegen die Sioux-Indianer. 1900 erschien sein Buch "History of Minnesota and Tales of the Frontier". Viele weitere Schriften, die heute von der Minnesota Historical Society aufbewahrt werden, gehen ebenfalls auf sein Konto. Ein Park bei New Ulm trägt, wie der oben erwähnte Bach, seinen Namen, der deutschen Ursprungs ist, aber durch Falschschreibung später eine französisch klingende Schreibweise erhielt.

GERMAN LAKE	Becker County
GERMAN LAKE	Isanti County
GERMAN LAKE	Le Sueur County
GERMAN LAKE	Otter Tail County
GERMAN LAKE	Washington County
GNEISS LAKE	Cook County
GOLDSCHMIDT (GOLDSMITH) LAKE	Carver County
GOLDSCHMIDT (GOLDSMITH) LAKE	Le Sueur County
HABERMAN LAKE	Otter Tail County
HAUSMANN LAKE	Hennepin County
HEILBERGER LAKE	Otter Tail County
HOFFMAN LAKE	Isanti County
HOFFMAN LAKE	Otter Tail County
HOFFMAN MARSH	Waseca County
KARL SLOUGH	Big Stone County
KARL LAKE	Cook County
KEITZMAN SLOUGH	Grant County
KELLER LAKE	Ramsey County
KELLER LAKE	Todd County
KNAUS LAKE	Stearns County
KNIEFF LAKE	Crow Wing County
KNOBEL LAKE	Otter Tail County
KOHLMAN LAKE	Ramsey County
KRAEMER LAKE	Stearns County
KRAETZ LAKE	Hennepin County
KRAFT LAKE	Morrison County
KRAMER LAKES	Pine County
KRANTZ LAKE	Pope County
KRANZ LAKE	Stearns County

KRATZKE LAKE	Carver County
KRAUT LAKE	Cook County
KRAUT LAKE	Becker County
KREIGLE LAKE	Stearns County
KREMER LAKE	Itasca County
KRENZ LAKE	Scott County
KRONE LAKE	Isanti County
KRUGER LAKE	Brown County

Situated in Prairieville Township, it was named after a German farmer, Louis Krüger.

In der Township Prairieville gelegen, benannt nach dem deutschen Farmer Louis Krüger.

KUHTZ LAKE	Douglas County
LAGER LAKE	Todd County
LAKE HUMMEL	Brown County
LAKE JUNI	Brown County

This lake was named after Benedict Juni from New Ulm and lies in Sigel Township. Born in Switzerland in 1852 he came to America at the age of five. In 1862 for a time he was a prisoner of the Sioux. Later his experiences as such were described in the "History of Brown County". Juni served more than 30 years as a teacher in a rural school.

In der Township Sigel, benannt nach Benedict Juni aus New Ulm. In der Schweiz 1852 geboren, kam er mit fünf Jahren nach Amerika. 1862 war er für einige Zeit Gefangener der Sioux. Seine Erlebnisse schilderte er später in der "History of Brown County". Juli diente mehr als 30 Jahre als Lehrer an Dorfschulen.

LAKE KEMPFER	Otter Tail County
LAKE KIESTER	Martin County
LANGE MARSH	Murray County
LEITHEISER LAKE	Becker County
LEMMERHIRT, NORTH and SOUTH (LAKE)	Otter Tail County
LIEBERG LAKE	Blue Earth County
LODEMEIER LAKE	Morrison County
LORRAINE LAKE	Itasca County
MANN LAKE	Cass County
MANN LAKE	Washington County
MAUSER LAKE	Cook County
MEUWISSEN LAKE	Carver County
MEYER LAKE	Crow Wing County
MEYER LAKE	Otter Tail County
MEYERS LAKE	Stearns County
MEYERS LAKE	Todd County

MILLER'S LAKE   Carver County
In Carver County, on Section 8, Dahlgren Township. Named in honor of Hermann
Müller.
*In der Sektion 8 der Township Dahlgren gelegen, nach dem Siedler Hermann Müller
benannt.*

MILLER LAKE		Carlton County
MILLER LAKE	(1)	Crow Wing County
MILLER LAKE	(2)	Crow Wing County
MILLER LAKE	(1)	Itasca County
MILLER LAKE	(2)	Itasca County
MILLER LAKE		Meeker County
MILLER LAKE		Pine County
MILLER LAKE		Wadena County
MINZER LAKE		Itasca County
NAGEL LAKE		Hubbard County
NAGEL LAKE		Itasca County
NEUMANN LAKE		Otter Tail County
NEUNER LAKE		Becker County
OPPERMAN LAKE		Otter Tail County
OSTERBERG LAKE		Pope County
OTTO LAKE		Cook County
OTTO LAKE		St. Louis County
PFEIFFER LAKE		St. Louis County
PIERZ LAKE		Cook County
PIERZ LAKE		Morrisson County
RAUSCH LAKE		Stearns County
REGENBOGEN LAKE		St. Louis County
REICH LAKE		McLeod County
REINKE SLOUGH		Blue Earth County
REITZ LAKE		Carver County
RETZLAFF (RETZHOFF) LAKE		Grant County
RHINE LAKE		Pine County
ROHRBECK LAKE		Meeker County

RUTZ LAKE   Carver County
Named for Peter Rutz, the first settler in the area.
*Nach einem gewissen Peter Rutz benannt, der wohl als erster in dieser Gegend
siedelte.*

SAUER LAKE	Becker County
SAUER LAKE	Otter Tail County

SCHACKMAN LAKE	Stearns County
SCHAEFFER LAKE	St. Louis County
SCHAFER LAKE	Todd County
SCHAFFER LAKE	Crow Wing County
SCHANTZEN LAKE	Clearwater County
SCHAUER LAKE	Hennepin County
SCHENDEL LAKE	Hennepin County
SCHIELENS LAKE	St. Louis County
SCHILLING LAKE	Sibley County
SCHINN LAKE	St. Louis County
SCHISLER LAKE	St. Louis County
SCHLAMM LAKE	St. Louis County
SCHLESKE LAKE	Otter Tail County
SCHMIDT LAKE	Otter Tail County
SCHMIDTS LAKE	Wright County
SCHMITT LAKE	Dakota County
SCHNAPPAUF (SCHWAPPAUF) LAKE	Hennepin County
SCHNEIDER LAKE	Mahnomen County
SCHNEIDER LAKE	Polk County
SCHNEIDER LAKE	Scott County
SCHROEDER LAKE	Stearns County
SCHUBERT LAKE	St. Louis County
SCHULTZ LAKE	Becker County
SCHULTZ LAKE	Douglas County
SCHULTZ LAKE	Kandiyohi County
SCHULTZ LAKE	Meeker County
SCHULTZ LAKE	Carver County
SCHUMAN (SCHMID) LAKE	Stearns County

SCHUTZ LAKE   Carver County
Situated in Laketown Township and named in honor of Matthias Schütz. Schutz Lake on some maps is also called Goldschmidt Lake.
In der Township Laketown gelegen und nach einem gewissen Matthias Schütz benannt. Auf einigen Karten auch als Goldschmidt Lake verzeichnet.

SCHWING HAMME LAKE   Stearns County

SIEBER'S CREEK   Clay County
Named for Rudolf Sieber, local owner of a dairy farm.
Benannt nach Rudolf Sieber, der dort eine Milchfarm betrieb.

SIEGFRIED CREEK   Clearwater County
Named for A. H. Siegfried, a reporter for the Louisville Courrier-Journal.

Benannt nach einem ehemaligen Berichterstatter des Louisville Courrier-Journal, A. H. Siegfried.

SPINDLER LAKE   Becker County

SPITZER LAKE   Otter Tail County

STAHL LAKE   McLeod County
Named for the German-American farmer, Charles Stahl, who settled nearby in June, 1857.
Benannt nach dem deutschstämmigen Farmer Charles (Karl) Stahl, der hier im Juni 1857 siedelte.

STEMMER LAKE   Otter Tail County

STIEGER LAKE   Carver County
Named for Carl Stieger who farmed near the lake.
Benannt nach dem Siedler Carl Stieger, der nahe dieses Sees eine Farm betrieb.

STOCKHOUSEN LAKE   Douglas County
An adulterated name entered on offical maps to commemorate Hans G. von Stackhausen who held the first homestead here in 1879.
Der Name des Sees wurde in veränderter Form in die amtlichen Karten übertragen, er soll an Hans G. von Stackhausen erinnern, der als erster hier in dieser Gegend um 1879 eine Heimstätte errichtete.

SWEITZER (SCHWEITZER) LAKE   Hubbard County

THIELKE LAKE   Big Stone County

UHLENKOTT'S LAKE   Stearns County

UNDERBERG LAKE   Polk County

WAGNER LAKE   Itasca County

WAGNER LAKE   Otter Tail County

WAGNER LAKE   Wright County

WALSFELD LAKE   Hennepin County

WALTHAUSEN LAKE   Pine County

WAMBACH LAKE   Mahnomen County

WARBURG LAKE   Itasca County

WASSERMAN LAKE   Carver County
The name comes from Michael Wassermann, first settler in the area.
Namensgeber für diesen See war der erste Siedler in dieser Gegend, Michael Wassermann.

WEISEL CREEK   Fillmore County
Named for David Weisel who established a sawmill here at the mouth of the stream in 1855. On August 4, 1866 the entire mill was swept away in a flood in which Weisel and his entire family perished.
Benannt nach David Weisel, der 1855 hier ein Sägewerk und eine Mahlmühle an der Mündung des Baches errichtete. Die Mühle wurde bei einer Überschwemmung Anfang August 1866 von den Fluten weggerissen, David Weisel und seine ganze Familie ertranken.

WINKLER LAKE   Carver County
Named for Ignatz Winkler, apparently of South German origins.
Benannt nach Ignatz Winkler, der dem Namen nach aus dem süddeutschen Raum gestammt haben dürfte.

WINTERHALTER LAKE	Hennepin County
WOLSFELD LAKE	Hennepin County
YAEGER (JAEGER) LAKE	Wadena County
YAEGER (JAEGER) LAKE	Wright County
YODELER LAKE	St. Louis County
ZANDERS LAKE	Brown County
ZIMMER LAKE	Stearns County
ZIMMERMAN LAKE	Cass County
ZIPPEL BAY	Lake of the Woods

Note:
A lake may be listed more than once when it extends into another County.
Hinweis:
Der Name eines Sees kann mehr als einmal aufgelistet sein, wenn er sich über einen Landkreis hinaus erstreckt.

PHOTOGRAPH IDENTIFICATIONS
Zu den einzelnen Abbildungen

1. Berlin Township Hall.
2. The village of Berne, located on sections 17 and 18 in Dodge County along Highway 57 going north from Kasson and Mantorville.
3. Zwingli church with steeple in the village of Berne. Site of the annual Swiss festival held on the second Tuesday of August each year.
4. Bismarck Township hall on section 2 in Sibley County north of the town of Winthrop which lies on Highway 19.
5. Cemetery at the Lutheran church about two miles southwest of the Bismarck Township hall in Sibley County.
6. Grave marker "Krueger" in the cemetery near the Township hall of Bismarck.
7. Cologne lies on sections 11, 12, 13, and 14 in Anthony Township of Carver County.
8. An old broken down store in the village of Gotha where once a branch of a plant from the small town of Cologne, north of there had established a substation.
9. Cologne water tower in Carver County.
10. The small town of Danube located along Highway 212 on section 6 in Renville County.
11. The Danube, Minnesota Farmer's Elevator Company selling feeds and supplies to farmers in the area.
12. Danube Creamery, now closed, where once farmers delivered their milk in cans for processing to butter.
13. Sign in the center of Essig, explaining the history of the village.
14. Essig village sign located on section 19 in Milford Township in Brown County.
15. The community of Flensburg lies in sections 35 and 36 of Culdrum Township in Morrison County just south of Highway 28 running west from Little Falls.
16. The community of Flensburg has several taverns, one being served here by a sales representative from the Budweiser company.
17. The post office in Flensburg is housed in a gas station.
18. Flensburg is economically driven by its co-op creamery which now is primarily a feed and farm supply center.
19. The Catholic church in Flensburg.
20. Gravestone in the cemetery at Flensburg points both to the use of Polish as the local language and also to the importance of the place of death of this pastor.
21. Sign for the town of Fulda located on Highways 2 and 59 on sections 25 and 26 of Murray County in western Minnesota. The city was founded by Archbishop Ireland to accommodate settlers of German birth and descent then living in the crowded cities on the United States eastern seabord.
22. Home of the local newspaper in the town of Fulda.
23. U.S. post office in the town of Fulda.
24. Railroad depot of Fulda, with a hint of German style in its construction.
25. The municipal liquor sales outlet in downtown Fulda.

26. Fulda Community Center, now used especially for gatherings of the senior citizens (over 65).
27. Germantown Township hall located on section 29 in Cottonwood County, lying four miles west of Highway 71 north of Storden and Jeffers.
28. Gotha lies in sections 1, 2, 35 and 36 of Townships Hancock and Benton in Carver County. The main highways through it are 50 and 53.
29. Hamburg is a small town lying on Highway 50 in sections 28 and 33 of Young America Township in Carver County.
30. U.S. post office in Hamburg.
31. State Bank in Hamburg.
32. Chamber of Commerce sign near the entrance to the downtown of Hanover.
33. Hanover municipal Fire Department.
34. City of Hanover in Frankfort Township in Wright County.
35. Heidelberg city limit sign. A small village located on sections 19 and 20 in Lanesburgh Township of Le Sueur County. Highway 30 runs north-south through it.
36. The community of Klossner is located on section 3 in Courtland Township of Nicollet County along Highway 15 a few miles north of New Ulm.
37. Moltke Township hall on section 15 in Sibley County just north of Gibbon, named for the German General Helmut Count von Moltke (1800-1891), who directed the war of Prussia against France in 1870-71.
38. Gravestones in a cemetery near the community Lutheran Church and Township hall of Moltke in Sibley County.
39. New Germany sign along the railroad at the outskirts of the city.
40. The community of New Germany lies on Highway 30 west of Minneapolis in sections 4 and 5 of Camden Township in Carver County.
41. U.S. post office in New Germany, Carver County.
42. New Munich is located on sections 18 and 19 in Oak Township of Stearns County. The community lies on Highway 237 west of Interstate 94 northwest of St. Cloud.
43. The New Munich Creamery, where formerly farmers of the region delivered their milk and cream in cans to make butter.
44. New Munich sign.
45. Ten Commandment stone on the lawn of the Catholic Sacred Heart School in New Munich.
46. New Munich. The bank has its sign in the foreground, while the water tower with the town's name stands in the background.
47. With the water tower bearing the name and zip code of New Munich, the tavern in the foreground boasts service of Munich Hofbräu beer.
48. Sign at the entrance to the city of New Ulm in Brown County.
49. Sign on a New Ulm street indicating direction to Flandrau State Park, with Herman statue in the background.
50. New Ulm. Herman the Cheruscan Monument, a replica of the Teutoburger Forest Monument.
51. Mr. Dannheim's dairy store, called the "Kuhstall" to play on the German background of the family and community of New Ulm.
52. Domeier's German Store in downtown New Ulm, where sales consist almost exclusively of wares imported from Germany.
53. Sign post on the corner of the lot on which the Domeier store is located in downtown New Ulm.
54. Liquor store on Highway 15 in the southern part of the city of New Ulm.
55. Sign indicating direction to reach Herman statue and park with German style architecture of the former post office, now the Brown County museum.

56. Entrance to Dr. Martin Luther College with Herman Monument in the background.
57. New Ulm. The building called "Messerschmidt", once a restaurant by the same name, now housing a Chinese eating establishment.
58. Sign on road leading westward out of New Ulm with indication of attractions, including two parks, one called Harman, the other Hermann Heights.
59. Sign for the village of Opole, named for the upper Silesian city of Oppeln, here written with the Polish spelling, attesting to the language used by the immigrants here. Opole is located on Highway 17 about five miles west of the Mississippi River, some 20 miles northwest of St. Cloud.
60. Cemetery with German names on recent graves of deceased members of St. Luke's Church at Posen.
61. St. Luke's Lutheran Missouri Synod Church on section 22 in Yellow Medicine ca. one mile from the Posen Township hall.
62. Posen Township hall.
63. The village of Potsdam located on sections 11 and 12 in Farmington Township in Olmsted County, situated on Highway 247 northeast of Rochester.
64. Sigel Township hall, located in southeast central Brown County.
65. Baseball park sign along Highway 24 in Stark Township of Brown County.
66. Sign on the bleechers commemorating the donation of land by the Rothmeier family which originated in 'Kreis Bischofteinitz' in western Bohemia and lived in Stark Township in Brown County.

1. *Gemeindehaus der Township Berlin.*
2. *Die Ortschaft Berne in Sektion 17 und 18 in Dodge County am Highway 57, der von Kasson und Mantorville nordwärts führt.*
3. *Die Zwingli-Kirche mit charakteristischem Glockenturm in der Ortschaft Berne, in dem alljährlich am zweiten Dienstag im August ein Schweizer Volksfest abgehalten wird.*
4. *Gemeindehaus der Township Bismarck in Sektion 2 im Landkreis Sibley nördlich von Winthrop am Highway 19.*
5. *Friedhof bei der lutheranischen Kirche in der Township Bismarck (Sibley County) etwa zwei Meilen südwestlich des Gemeindehauses.*
6. *Grabstein der Auguste Krueger im Friedhof von Bismarck.*
7. *Cologne liegt in den Sektionen 11 bis 14 in der Anthony Township von Carver County.*
8. *Ein altes baufälliges Geschäftshaus in der Ortschaft Gotha, wo früher eine Werksfiliale des nördlicher gelegenen Cologne eingerichtet war.*
9. *Der Wasserturm von Cologne in der Carver County.*
10. *Die Kleinstadt Danube (= Donau) am Highway 212 in der Sektion 6 in Renville County.*
11. *Die „Getreidespeicher-Gesellschaft" der Farmer von Danube (eine Art landwirtschaftliche Genossenschaft), die an die Bauern in der Region Futtermittel und Versorgungsgüter verkauft.*
12. *Die stillgelegte Molkerei von Danube, wo früher die Farmer ihre Milch in Kannen ablieferten zum Zweck der Butterproduktion.*
13. *Hinweistafel im Zentrum von Essig mit Darstellung der Geschichte des Ortes.*
14. *Hinweisschild auf die Ortschaft Essig in der Sektion 19 der Milford Township im Landkreis Brown.*
15. *Die Gemeinde Flensburg liegt in den Sektionen 35 und 36 der Township Culdrum in Morrison County knapp südlich des Highway 28, der von Westen aus Richtung Little Falls herführt.*
16. *Die Gemeinde Flensburg besitzt mehrere Schankwirtschaften. Hier wird eben eine von einer Vertretung der Bierbrauerei Budweiser bedient.*

17. *Das Postamt von Flensburg ist in einer Tankstelle untergebracht.*
18. *Die Konsummolkerei von Flensburg, heute vornehmlich ein landwirtschaftliches Lagerhaus, bestimmt das Wirtschaftsleben in dieser Gemeinde.*
19. *Die katholische Kirche in Flensburg.*
20. *Dieser Grabstein auf dem Flensburger Friedhof weist auf den Gebrauch des Polnischen als Lokalsprache wie auch auf die Bedeutung der Sterbestätte dieses Pfarrers hin.*
21. *Ortschild von Fulda an den Highways 2 und 59 in der Murray County West-Minnesotas. Die Stadt wurde von Erzbischof Ireland gegründet, um Siedlern deutscher Abstammung aus den überfüllten Städten der amerikanischen Ostküste ein neues Heim zu geben.*
22. *Geschäftshaus der Lokalzeitung von Fulda.*
23. *Postgebäude von Fulda.*
24. *Bahnhofsgebäude von Fulda mit deutschen Architekturansätzen.*
25. *Städtisches Spirituosengeschäft im Zentrum von Fulda.*
26. *Das Gemeindehaus von Fulda, das jetzt vorwiegend für Seniorenversammlungen (über 65 Jahre) dient.*
27. *Gemeinderathaus der Township Germantown in der Sektion 29 von Cottonwood County, vier Meilen westlich des Highway 71 und nördlich von Storden und Jeffers.*
28. *Gotha liegt in vier Sektionen der Townships Hancock und Benton im Kreis Carver. Die Hauptstraßen 50 und 53 durchqueren den Ort.*
29. *Das kleine Städtchen Hamburg liegt am Highway 50 in der Township Young America (Carver County).*
30. *Postamt in Hamburg.*
31. *Staatsbank in Hamburg.*
32. *Hinweisschild der Handelskammer von Hanover am Eingang zum Ortszentrum.*
33. *Städtisches Feuerwehrhaus in Hanover.*
34. *Am Ortseingang von Hanover in der Township Frankfort (Wright County).*
35. *Ortsschild von Heidelberg, einem Dorf in der Lanesburgh Township des Kreises Le Sueur. Der Highway 30 verläuft in Nord-Süd-Richtung durch den Ort.*
36. *Die Gemeinde Klossner liegt in der Sektion 3 der Courtland Township in Nicollet County am Highway 15, der von New Ulm heraufführt.*
37. *Gemeindehaus (Rathaus) der Township Moltke in der Sibley County knapp nördlich von Gibbon. Die Township wurde nach Helmut Graf von Moltke (1800 - 1891) benannt, dem berühmten Generalfeldmarschall aus dem Krieg von 1870 - 71.*
38. *Grabsteine auf dem Friedhof in der Nähe der lutheranischen Gemeindekirche und des Gemeindehauses der Township Moltke in Sibley County.*
39. *Hinweisschild auf New Germany am Bahnkörper am Rande des Städtchens.*
40. *Die Gemeinde New Germany liegt am Highway 30 westlich von Minneapolis in der Camden Township von Carver County.*
41. *Das Postgebäude von New Germany in der Carver County.*
42. *New Munich liegt in den Sektionen 18 und 19 der Township Oak in Stearns County. Der Highway 237 führt von der Schnellstraße 'Interstate 94' westlich zu der kleinen Gemeinde; St. Cloud liegt südöstlich.*
43. *Die Molkerei von New Munich, wo früher die Farmer des Umlandes Milch und Rahm zur Buttererzeugung in Kannen anlieferten.*
44. *Ortsschild von New Munich.*
45. *Stein mit den „Zehn Geboten" auf dem Rasen vor der katholischen 'Sacred Heart'-Schule in New Munich.*
46. *New Munichs Hauptstraße mit der Werbetafel einer Bank im Vorder- und dem alles überragenden Wasserturm mit dem Namen des Ortes im Hintergrund.*

47. New Munich. Die Schankwirtschaft rühmt sich ihres Münchner Hofbräu-Bie-
res. Im Hintergrund der alles überragende Wasserturm mit der Postleitzahl.
48. Ortseingangsschild von New Ulm in Brown County.
49. Hinweisschild an einer Straße in New Ulm, das den Weg zum Flandrau-Park
zeigt. Im Hintergrund die Hermann-Statue.
50. Das Hermann-Denkmal in New Ulm, eine Nachbildung des Originals im Teutoburger Wald.
51. Dannheim-Milchgeschäft mit dem originellen Titel „Kuhstall", eine Anspie-
lung auf das deutsche Erbe der Familie und der Gemeinde New Ulm.
52. Domeier's Deutscher Laden im Zentrum von New Ulm, dessen Angebot fast
gänzlich aus deutscher Importware besteht.
53. Wegweiserpfahl auf dem Grundstück des Domeier-Ladens in der Ortsmitte
von New Ulm.
54. Spirituosengeschäft am Highway 15 im Südteil von New Ulm.
55. Wegweiser zu dem Hügel etwas außerhalb der Stadt, auf dem das Hermann-
Monument steht. Das Gebäude im Hintergrund, ehemals die Post, heute das
Museum des Landkreises Brown, trägt deutliche deutsche architektonische
Züge.
56. Eingang zum Dr.-Martin-Luther-College. Im Hintergrund das Hermann-Denkmal.
57. Haus Messerschmidt in New Ulm. Einst war es eine bekannte Speisegaststät-
te, heute beherbergt es ein China-Restaurant.
58. Dieser Wegweiser deutet auf eine Straße hin, die New Ulm in westlicher
Richtung verläßt und zu einigen Attraktionen führt, unter anderem zu zwei
Parkanlagen mit ähnlich klingenden Namen: Harman und Hermann.
59. Ortsschild von Opole. Hinter diesem polnischen Namen verbirgt sich die ehemalige deutsch-oberschlesische Stadt Oppeln. Opole ist ein deutlicher Hinweis auf die Sprache der Einwanderer. Es waren keine Deutschen, sondern
Polen. Opole liegt am Highway 17, etwa fünf Meilen westlich des noch jun-
gen Mississippi, einige zwanzig Meilen nordwestlich von St. Cloud.
60. Friedhof der St. Lukas-Kirche in Posen mit Grabsteinen aus der jüngeren
Vergangenheit.
61. Die evangelische Kirche der St. Lukas Missouri Synode in der Sektion 22 von
Yellow Medicine, etwa eine Meile vom Posener Township-Gemeindehaus entfernt.
62. Das Gemeindehaus von Posen Township.
63. Die Ortschaft Potsdam befindet sich in den Sektionen 11 und 12 der Township Farmington im Kreis Olmsted am Highway 247 nordöstlich von Rochester.
64. Rathaus der Sigel Township im südöstlichen zentralen Landkreis Brown.
65. Hinweisschild auf ein Baseballfeld am Highway 24 in der Township Stark in
Brown County.
66. Eine Tafel an den Rängen der nichtüberdachten Tribüne des Baseballstadions
in Stark besagt, daß der Grund, auf dem der Sportplatz steht, eine Schen-
kung der Rothmeier-Familie ist, die aus dem Kreis Bischofteinitz in West-
böhmen stammt und hier in Brown County ansässig wurde.

1. Berlin

2. Berne

3. Berne

4. Bismarck

5. Bismarck

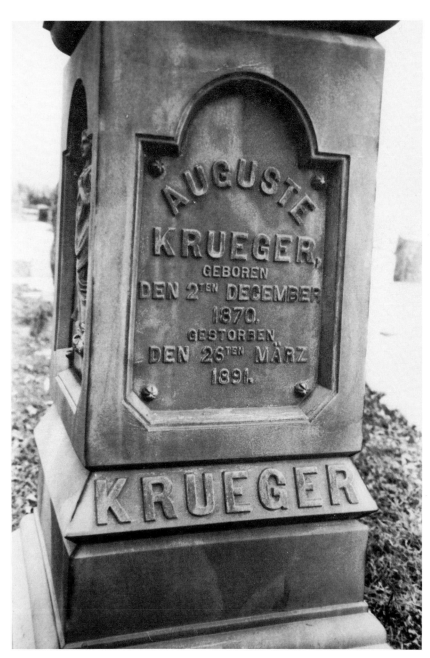

6. Bismarck

7. Cologne

8. Gotha

9. Cologne

10. Danube

11. Danube

12. Danube

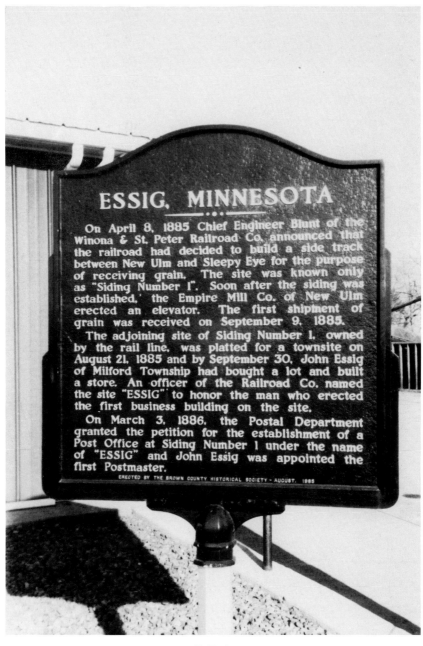

ESSIG, MINNESOTA

On April 8, 1885 Chief Engineer Blunt of the Winona & St. Peter Railroad Co. announced that the railroad had decided to build a side track between New Ulm and Sleepy Eye for the purpose of receiving grain. The site was known only as "Siding Number 1". Soon after the siding was established, the Empire Mill Co. of New Ulm erected an elevator. The first shipment of grain was received on September 9, 1885.

The adjoining site of Siding Number 1, owned by the rail line, was platted for a townsite on August 21, 1885 and by September 30, John Essig of Milford Township had bought a lot and built a store. An officer of the Railroad Co. named the site "ESSIG" to honor the man who erected the first business building on the site.

On March 3, 1886, the Postal Department granted the petition for the establishment of a Post Office at Siding Number 1 under the name of "ESSIG" and John Essig was appointed the first Postmaster.

ERECTED BY THE BROWN COUNTY HISTORICAL SOCIETY - AUGUST, 1985

13. Essig

14. Essig

15. Flensburg

16. Flensburg

17. Flensburg

18. Flensburg

19. Flensburg

TU SPOCZYWA Ś.P.
KS. ST. ŁĄCZYNSKI
PROBOSZCZ
W FLENSBURG
1863 — 1902

R.I.P.

Prosi o
zdrowaś maryo,

WDZIĘCZNI
PARAFIANIE

20. Flensburg

21. Fulda

22. Fulda

23. Fulda

24. Fulda

25. Fulda

26. Fulda

27. Germantown

28. Gotha

29. Hamburg

30. Hamburg

31. Hamburg

32. Hannover

33. Hannover

34. Hannover

35. Heidelberg

36. Klossner

37. Moltke

38. Moltke

39. New Germany

40. New Germany

41. New Germany

42. New Munich

43. New Munich

44. New Munich

the Ten Commandments

I AM the LORD thy God.

I. Thou shalt have no other gods before me.
II. Thou shalt not take the Name of the Lord thy God in vain.
III. Remember the Sabbath day, to keep it holy.
IV. Honor thy father and thy mother, that thy days may be long upon the land which the Lord thy God giveth thee.
V. Thou shalt not kill.
VI. Thou shalt not commit adultery.
VII. Thou shalt not steal.
VIII. Thou shalt not bear false witness against thy neighbor.
IX. Thou shalt not covet thy neighbor's house.
X. Thou shalt not covet thy neighbor's wife, nor his manservant nor his maidservant, nor his cattle, nor anything that is thy neighbors.

DEDICATED TO
THEIR CHILDREN AND FUTURE
GENERATIONS OF NEW MUNICH
BY
MR. AND MRS. NORBERT FUNK
1957

45. New Munich

46. New Munich

47. New Munich

56. New Ulm

57. New Ulm

58. New Ulm

59. Opole

60. Posen

61. Posen

62. Posen

63. Potsdam

64. Sigel

65. Stark

66. Stark

ABOUT THE AUTHORS
Über die Autoren

La Vern J. Rippley is a professor of German and German historical topics at St. Olaf College in Northfield, Minnesota where he has taught since 1967. Professor Rippley was born in 1935 in Wisconsin of ancestors on his paternal side from the village of Unadingen near Donaueschingen in Baden who emigrated around 1855 with the name Rieple. His maternal ancestry is from the eastern German village of Poppelau near Oppeln in Upper Silesia, since 1945 under Polish rule.

Rippley attended schools in Waumandee, Wisconsin before studying at Kent State and the Ohio State University where he took his Ph.D. in 1965. In the years 1963 - 64 he was a Fulbright Fellow at the University of Munich. Before coming to St. Olaf College in Minnesota he was a professor at Ohio State and for three years at Ohio Wesleyan University in Delaware, Ohio.

The author of eight other books including **Of German Ways** (1970), **The German-Americans** (1976), **Excursions Through America** (1973), **Russian-German Settle-**

ments in the United States (1974) and **The Immigrant Experience in Wisconsin** (1985), Rippley has written over 100 scholarly articles for various journals and hundreds of book reviews. He also edits the **Newsletter** of the Society for German-American Studies.

The project on German place names in Minnesota was initiated by Rainer H. Schmeissner of Regensburg, Bavaria. Perhaps it is of interest that in the United States, a nation which today has more people reporting ancestry from Germany than from any other nation on the globe, does not in fact have **more** place names of German origin. The reason for the relatively small number of such names is no doubt due to the fact that the system of government in the United States from its outset was and remains basically English. Secondly, it was the original American-born surveyors who as a rule gave names to the local regions irrespective of the people who would eventually live there. Thus in cases where German names were actually entered on the maps, it took a special initiative on the part of the new-comers to re-name sites so that their own preferences in titling locations resulted in evidence of their origins, e. g. town building by German immigrants where once no town had been envisioned.

Rippley's responsibility was the English version along with photographs for the sites included here. In some cases the name of a place was nowhere officially in evidence. While maps or common local agreement gave a lake or stream a name of German origin, for example, there was no public sign or item on the landscape to identify it specifically as German. Thus the photographs are limited to public displays and do not entirely reflect regions that are the most German either in original population or present influence. Still, it is phenomenal how many German names do speckle the county maps of Minnesota. This book is intended to exemplify this fact and to enrich the reader's appreciation for the state's German immigrants of a century ago.

La Vern J. Rippley ist Professor für Deutsch und Deutsche Geschichtsthematik am St. Olaf College in Northfield, Minnesota, wo er seit 1967 unterrichtet. Professor Rippley wurde 1935 in Wisconsin geboren; seine Vorfahren väterlicherseits stammen aus dem Ort Unadingen bei Donaueschingen in Baden, die um 1855 unter dem Namen Rieple auswanderten. Aus dem ostdeutschen Ort Poppelau bei Oppeln in Oberschlesien (seit 1945 unter polnischer Verwaltung) kommen die Angehörigen mütterlicherseits.

Rippley besuchte Schulen in Waumandee (Wisconsin), bevor er an der Kent State und der Ohio State Universität studierte, wo er 1965 zum Doktor der Philosophie promovierte. In den Jahren 1963 - 64 brachte ihn ein Fulbright Stipendium an die Universität nach München. Bevor er an das St. Olaf College in Minnesota gerufen wurde, war er Professor an der Ohio State und dann drei Jahre lang an der Ohio Wesleyan Universität in Delaware, Ohio.

Der Autor von acht weiteren Büchern, darunter Of German Ways (Über das Deutschtum; 1970), The German-Americans (Die Deutsch-Amerikaner; 1976), Excursions Through America (Reisen durch Amerika; 1973), Russian-German Settlements in the United States (Rußlanddeutsche Siedlungen in den Vereinigten Staaten; 1974) und The Immigrant Experience in Wisconsin (Die Einwanderung in Wisconsin unter den Aspekten der Erfahrung und der Erlebnisse; 1985) schrieb darüber hinaus über hundert wissenschaftliche Beiträge für verschiedene Schriftenreihen und Hunderte von Buchrezensionen. Er zeichnet auch als Herausgeber des Newsletter, einem Mitteilungsblatt der Gesellschaft für Deutsch-Amerikanische Studien.

Das Projekt „Deutsche Ortsnamen in Minnesota" wurde von Rainer H. Schmeissner aus Regensburg initiiert. Es dürfte wahrscheinlich von Interesse sein, daß es in den Vereinigten Staaten trotz der Tatsache, daß dort mehr Menschen eine deutsche Ahnenschaft nachweisen können als jede andere Volksgruppe, de facto nicht noch **mehr** Ortsnamen deutschen Ursprungs gibt. Der Grund für die relativ kleine Zahl solcher Namen (in Bezug auf die Gesamtzahl der Ortsnamen) ist zweifellos darin zu suchen, daß das Regierungssystem in den Vereingten Staaten von Anfang an englisch war und ist. Zum anderen gaben die bereits im Lande geborenen Geometer in der Regel den lokalen Örtlichkeiten Namen, die unabhängig waren von der Herkunft der später hier lebenden Siedler. In den Fällen, wo deutsche Namen tatsächlich in die Landkarte eingetragen wurden, bedurfte es besonderer Initiative von seiten der Neuankömmlinge, Stätten so umzubenennen, daß darin ihre ethnische Herkunft zum Tragen kam. Dies traf vor allem auf Ortsgründungen von deutschen Einwanderern zu, die an Plätzen geschahen, wo zunächst keine Siedlung vorgesehen worden war.

Rippley zeichnet verantwortlich für die englische Fassung zusammen mit den Fotografien der in diesem Buch vorgestellten Orte mit deutschen Namen. In einigen Fällen war an Plätzen mit deutschen Ortsnamen die Bezeichnung offiziell nicht sichtbar. Dies trifft vor allem auf Gewässernamen zu, die zwar auf Landkarten oder im lokalen Gebrauch auf deutschen Ursprung schließen lassen, dies aber nicht durch ein Hinweisschild in der Landschaft sichtbar dokumentieren. So sind die Fotografien auf öffentliche Ortstafeln und Hinweisschilder begrenzt, geben also nicht den tatsächlichen Stand von Gegenden wieder, die ursprünglich von Deutschen besiedelt wurden oder später deutschen Einflüssen unterlagen. Dennoch erscheint es außergewöhnlich, wie viele deutsche Namen die Landkarten von Minnesota übersäen. Die Aufgabe dieses Buches ist es, diese Tatsache zu veranschaulichen und das Verständnis des Lesers für die deutsche Einwanderung vor hundert Jahren zu wecken.

Rainer H. Schmeissner, head teacher at a school for special education in Bavaria, was born in 1946 in the small town of Marktleuthen on the Eger River in Northern Bavaria. Schmeissner attended elementary and high schools in Regensburg, which is located in the heart of Bavaria. From 1968 until 1971 he studied at the Teachers' College in Regensburg and from 1972 until 1974 at the University of Munich.

Already at an early period in his career, Schmeissner was active in research concerning monuments of various types. He was co-founder of a local study group in the Upper Palatinate and today serves as president of an international research cooperative called "Steinkreuzforschung". In addition to dozens of contributions and shorter essays, he has written numerous books on this topic, for example, **Der Burgfrieden der ehemals freien Reichsstadt Regensburg** (Fortress Jurisdictional Boundary Markers

for the Former Imperial City of Regensburg; 1976), **Westnordische Kreuzsteine** (Cross Slabs on the Isles Northwest of Scotland; 1976), **Steinkreuze in der Oberpfalz** (Stone Crosses in the Upper Palatinate; 1977), **Ölands Kulturdenkmäler in Fluren und Kirchhöfen** (Öland's Cultural Monuments in Field and Churchyard; 1978), **Kirchen, Kreuze und Runen auf den Färöern** (The Churches, Crosses and Runes of the Faroes; 1979), **Schweizer Rechtsdenkmäler** (Monuments of a Legal Nature in Switzerland; 1980), and **Oberpfälzer Flurdenkmäler** (Open Field Monuments of the Upper Palatinate; 1986).

Besides his many writings on the local history and geography of his immediate home region, the Fichtel Mountains, Schmeissner is the publisher and editor of three journals.

Since his earliest scholarly awakening, Schmeissner has been interested in the geography of Northern Europe and North America. Between 1972 and 1987 he visited all of the Scandinavian countries, including Iceland and Greenland, as well as major portions of the American Middle West and the Canadian Northwest. Schmeissner has written books on this complex of places, such as **Die Färöer - Inselwelt im Nordatlantik** (The Faroes - An Island World in the North Atlantic; 1983), **Die Black Hills von Süddakota** (1987), **Norddakota - Präriestaat im Norden Amerikas** (1987), **Ostgrönland** (East Greenland; 1987), **Der Mackenzie Highway** (1988), **High Level, Alberta** (1988), and **True West - Wo der Westen beginnt** (True West - Where the West Begins; 1989).

The author offers proof of his special love for Minnesota with his two publications **Minnesota - Land des himmelfarbenen Wassers** (Minnesota - Land of Sky Blue Waters; 1986) and **Runen in Amerika? Die Geschichte des Kensington-Steins von Minnesota** (1988).

The instigation for this book about German place names in Minnesota was generated through a visit of Professor La Vern J. Rippley to Regensburg in 1988. The suggestion came to fruition through mutual cooperation.

Rainer H. Schmeissner, Oberlehrer an einer bayerischen Sonderschule, wurde 1946 in der Kleinstadt Marktleuthen an der Eger in Nordbayern geboren. Die Volksschule und das Gymnasium besuchte Schmeissner in Regensburg. Von 1968 bis 1971 studierte er an der Pädagogischen Hochschule in Regensburg und von 1972 bis 1974 an der Universität in München.

Sehr früh engagierte sich Schmeissner für die Belange der Denkmalforschung. Als Mitbegründer eines regionalen Arbeitskreises in der Oberpfalz ist er heute Vorsitzender einer internationalen Forschervereinigung (Steinkreuzforschung). Neben Dutzenden von Beiträgen und kleinen Schriften schrieb er auch zahlreiche Bücher zu diesem Thema, z.B. Der Burgfrieden der ehemals freien Reichsstadt Regensburg (1976), Westnordische Kreuzsteine (1976), Steinkreuze in der Oberpfalz (1977), Ölands Kulturdenkmale in Fluren und Kirchhöfen (1978), Kirchen, Kreuze und Runen auf den Färöern (1979), Schweizer Rechtsdenkmäler (1980), Steinkreuze in Schweden (1984) und Oberpfälzer Flurdenkmäler (1986).

Neben zahlreichen Schriften zur Heimatkunde seiner Heimat Fichtelgebirge zeichnet Schmeissner als Herausgeber von drei Schriftenreihen.

Sein besonderes Interesse galt darüberhinaus von jeher der Geographie Nordeuropas und Amerikas. Zwischen 1972 und 1987 besuchte er sämtliche skandinavischen Länder einschließlich Island und Grönland sowie weite Teile des amerikanischen Mittleren Westens und des kanadischen Nordwestens. Zu diesem Themenkreis verfaßte Schmeissner Bücher wie: Die Färöer - Inselwelt im Nordatlantik (1983), Öland - Schwedens kleinste Provinz (1984), Die Black Hills von Süddakota (1987),

Norddakota - Präriestaat im Norden Amerikas (1987), **Ostgrönland** *(1987)*, **Der Mackenzie Highway** *(1988)*, **High Level, Alberta** *(1988)* und **True West - Wo der Westen beginnt** *(1989)*.

Seine besondere Liebe zu Minnesota dokumentierte der Verfasser durch die beiden Schriften **Minnesota – Land des himmelfarbenen Wassers** *(1986)* und **Runen in Amerika? Die Geschichte des Kensington-Steins von Minnesota** *(1988)*.

Die Idee zu einem Ortsverzeichnis deutscher Namen in Minnesota kam anläßlich eines Besuchs von Professor La Vern J. Rippley in Regensburg (1988). Sie wurde von Professor Rippley dankbar aufgegriffen und in gemeinschaftlicher Zusammenarbeit in die Tat umgesetzt.

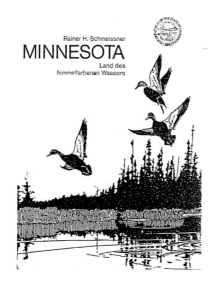

106